LOIS M. WILSON

I Want to Be in That Number

Cool Saints I Have Known

For Kathy Brown –
Lois M. Wilson

Edited by Jean Wilson
Illustrations by Jane Casson

Published in 2014 by
The Very Rev. Dr. the Hon. Lois M. Wilson, CC
6canoe@gmail.com

© Copyright 2014 by
The Very Rev. Dr. the Hon. Lois M. Wilson, CC

All rights reserved. No part of this book may be reproduced by any means without the written permission of the publisher.

Second printing May 2015 · Printed in Canada

Cataloguing data available from Library and Archives Canada

Lois M. Wilson, 1927–
"I Want to Be in That Number"
ISBN 978-0-9780839-1-5

Table of Contents

5   Abbreviations

7   Introduction

Chapter 1 *Justice*

12	Bührig, Dr. Marga	Germany
16	Burnett, Rev. P. Stephen	United Kingdom
20	Daniel, Rev. Harry F.J.	India
24	Endicott, Rev. James Gareth	Canada and China
28	Heap, Alice Mildred (Boomhour)	Canada
32	Kim, Dae-Jung, President	South Korea (ROK)
36	Legge, Rev. Dr. Garth Warren	Canada
40	Naudé, Rev. Dr. C.F. Beyers	South Africa
44	Oh, Jae Shik	South Korea (ROK)
48	Santiso, Dr. Maria Theresa Porcile	Uruguay

Chapter 2 *Resurrection*

54	Bonino, Rev. Dr. José Miguez	Argentina
58	Cummings, Marjorie Davis (Freeman)	Canada
61	Elliott, Rev. Dr. Clifford A.S. Elliott	Canada
65	Freeman, Rev. Dr. E. Gardner (Gard) D.	Canada
69	Laurence, Dr. Jean Margaret	Canada
74	Lind, Alexander Udny	Canada
77	McMahon, Bertha Margaret	Canada
82	Sölle, Dr. Dorothee	Germany
87	Tillman, Frances (Frankie) Geddes Montgomery	Canada
91	Ting, Bishop K.H. (Ting Kuang-hsun)	China

CHAPTER 3 *Transformation*

96	Barrow, Dame Ruth Nita	Barbados
100	Freeman, Verna Isabel (Margaret)	Canada
104	Hockin, Dr. Katherine Boehner	Canada
108	Jackman, Dr. Mary Coyne Rowell	Canada
112	Mutch, Anne Gertrude	Canada
116	Norrie, William (Bill)	Canada
120	Scott, The Most Rev. Edward (Ted) Walter	Canada
124	Siwallace, Mary Lynn (Mooney)	Canada
128	Whitehead, Dr. Rhea Menzel	Canada
132	Wilson, Rev. Dr. Roy Fyfe	Canada

CHAPTER 4 *Church and the World*

138	Carrel, John Beaton Laughton	Canada
142	Cotton, J. Robert (Rob)	Canada
145	Freeman, Minnie Ada	Canada
149	Gibson, Robin	Canada
153	Harvey, John Gardner	Canada
157	Moore, The Very Rev. Dr. Arthur B.B.	Canada
161	Pagel, Barton (Bart) Louis	USA
165	Prang, Dr. Margaret Evelyn	Canada
169	Thomas, Dr. M.M.	India
173	Wyman, Rev. Harold Carlyle	Canada

177 *Conclusion*

Bergen-Belsen, Germany, 178; Hiroshima, Japan, 182; Kwangju, South Korea (ROK), 186

Abbreviations

CCC	Canadian Council of Churches OR China Christian Council
CCA	Christian Conference of Asia
KJV	King James Version of the Bible
NEB	New English Bible
NRSV	New Revised Standard Version of the Bible
PWRDF	The Primate's World Relief and Development Fund (Anglican Church of Canada)
RSV	Revised Standard Version of the Bible
SCM	Student Christian Movement
UN	United Nations
URM	Urban Rural Mission
VU	Voices United (The Hymn and Worship Book of the United Church of Canada)
WCC	World Council of Churches
WSCF	World Student Christian Federation
YWCA	Young Women's Christian Association

Brief Historical Background for a Number of the Biblical Texts

Many of the texts are the story of Jerusalem and its people after a long period of civil war. Eventually Israel was invaded by the Chaldeans who destroyed the first temple in Jerusalem, which was the centre of Israel's religious life. The Israelites were then sent on a long journey of exile to Babylon. Eventually King Cyrus of Persia facilitated their return and they rebuilt the Temple in Jerusalem. Many of the Biblical texts used in this book emerge out of this history of pain, dislocation, the destruction of war, and the intense longing to return home. The poetic visionary prophets foresee the reconstruction of a new society according to the laws and insights of Yahweh.

Introduction

I celebrated my 85th birthday in April, 2012 with a symposium on "Religion and Public Policy" at Emmanuel College in Toronto. I thought that was a better way of celebrating it than throwing a big dinner where we all ate lots and got much fatter. Three of my former World Council of Churches friends agreed, so they all used their frequent flyer points and came to the celebration. Bishop Bärbel Potter came from Germany; WCC President Ofelia Ortega from Cuba; and Dr. Jan Love from Atlanta Georgia. When I saw that friends from all generations were present and joining in the gathering, it gave me pause. The younger people had never heard the stories we told of what Christian life and witness were like globally in the world of the 1980s. Some did not catch our references to people who had made a salutary contribution to Christian community three or four decades ago—and how could they? They weren't even born at that time! I started to wonder if my own grandkids knew or even cared about the rich legacy some of my friends had contributed to the practice of justice and peace from our faith community. It prompted me to think about my own legacy. Did I have any insights about aging or faith to pass on to younger generations?

All of this came into focus one Sunday morning in the summer of 2012 while sitting on my patio overlooking Lake Superior. I had a conversation with my daughter Jean about a possible book I might write on aging and death. She suggested that one of my particular strengths, in her view, was my grounding in and knowledge of the Biblical text. Lots of people would have perspectives to share about aging, but she thought if I focused on Biblical texts, I might make a more lasting contribution. Then we got to talking about the significance of Biblical passages chosen for loved ones' funeral services. When I consulted my marked-up Bible, I noticed that when a loved or admired friend died, I had noted the date of their death opposite the scriptural text chosen for the funeral. I started with Genesis and flipped through my entire Bible, finding about forty-three such notations. Why had I done this over the years? I think it was my way of remembering their life and legacy every time I read that passage. It was a way of energizing myself and spurring me on to continue the work for justice and peace that the gospel calls forth. They were people who did not choose texts for their sentimental value or because the text was comforting to them. They or their families chose texts carefully to reflect their Christian life experience and spirituality. Jean recalled how impressed she had been when we visited Riverside Church in New York City, only to find alongside the photos of past ministers at the church quotations that indicated the specific orientation of these leaders in their faith and service. Could I do something similar?

When Jean and I hatched this book we discussed procedure. As a Comparative Literature professor at McMaster University, she regularly teaches ancient texts such as Homer's *Iliad* and *Odyssey*. Although I am no Biblical scholar, I know the texts of the Hebrew and Greek Bible, so I consulted with her about discerning the meaning of texts. We decided that I would identify each of these people to the reader by presenting a greatly condensed biography of their life; set them in their historical context; relate the scriptural texts used at their funeral to the work and witness of the person I had known; and then wrestle with the scriptural texts in such a way that the texts were seen to critique the world we have, as well as to create new possibilities for the world we would like to have. What could we learn from them? The point would be not to focus on what the intended meaning of the text was for the person who chose it, but to consider what meaning we can derive from it for our witness today. A daunting task, and not always fully accomplished!

It wasn't long before I realized I was writing about what the Apostles' Creed calls "the communion of saints." How many of my readers would care? How many would want to tap this rich resource of energy and spirituality? How many would appreciate the profound need of our highly individualistic culture and its denial of death to reconsider all that is implied about community and the nature of the church in that phrase "the communion of saints?" How many would appreciate how countercultural this affirmation of community is, in a society that produces books such as "Bowling Alone?"

I discovered that Dietrich Bonhoeffer had written his first dissertation *Sanctorum Communio* ("The Communion of Saints") on the nature of the church. He wrote it in 1927, the year of my birth, when he was only twenty-one. His thesis is that the Church is "Christ existing as community." The task is to discover the concrete Christian community in which the life of Christ takes shape. The unique nature of the church results from it being both divine and human, as was Jesus. When I attended an Anglican church, we remembered "the glorious company of the apostles, the fellowship of the prophets, the noble army of martyrs and the Holy Church throughout the world." That's what I was starting to write about.

Karen Hamilton, General Secretary of the Canadian Council of Churches, pointed out to me how N.T. Wright, in his book *How God Became King*, writes,

> Those who have gone before us include, especially, those who have lived, suffered, and died to bear witness to Jesus as the world's true Lord over against the other "lords" that try to claim our allegiance. To be "in communion" with them is far more than simply hoping that our departed loved ones will actually still, in some sense, be in touch with us, that there will be some kind of mystical contact beyond the grave. It is to share in the fellowship and solidarity with all those who have been the "kingdom people" of their day and to gain strength and courage from them for our own witness." It was highly significant, in view of the vocation he had already sensed, that Dietrich Bonhoeffer chose to write his doctoral dissertation, "Communion Sanctorum," on this clause.[1]

As Anglican Bishop K.H. Ting of China wrote in a personal letter to me on 10 Sept. 1994 on the death of our colleague Bishop Shin Yi-fan, quoting St. Symeon (949-1022), a mystical poet and theologian in Constantinople, "The saints in each generation, joined to those who have gone before and filled them with light, become a golden chain, in which each saint is a separate link, united to the next by faith and works and love. So, in the one God they form a single chain which cannot quickly be broken." Church history helps us see the endlessness of the procession of self-giving saints old and young, bringing their gifts to enrich the common life of the church.

As I reflected, general themes began to emerge, and I have grouped the articles around those themes: Justice; Resurrection; Transformation; Church and the World. You are invited to join me in my discoveries about our common Christian life and legacy.

I acknowledge my great debt to relatives and friends of the saints who freely provided information; to Sheryl Johnson, who reviewed early drafts; to Jean Wilson for careful editing; to Jane Casson for art work; and to Saskia Rowley for guiding the project through all stages of production. Without them, there would be no book.

Lois M. Wilson

---

1 N.T. Wright, *How God Became King: The Forgotten Story of the Gospels* (NY: HarperCollins, 2012), p. 271. By "clause," Wright is referring to the clause in the Apostles' Creed which refers to the Communion of Saints.

CHAPTER 1

Justice

Marga Bührig, Germany
1915 – 12 February 2002

Lay Feminist theologian; One of Founders of "Women for Peace" and Swiss Protestant Women's Federation; Director of Boldern Lay Academy ('59–'81); President of Laity Centres in Europe ('76–'82); One of three female Presidents of World Council of Churches ('83–'91); Chair of WCC conference on Justice, Peace, Integrity of Creation ('90).

"The only reason I didn't walk out was that all the Russian grandmothers were looking at me and smiling, and would not have understood why I felt like walking out," she told me. Marga's feminism was in full bloom when the WCC opened its meeting in Moscow with a communion service. Ninety-five percent of the congregation were women—mostly grandmothers. Yet the WCC had placed three men in the highly visible role of administering the sacrament. That contradicted what the Assembly had tried to do when, at Vancouver, it elected three women (including her) as part of a six person Presidium to be the public face of the WCC. Marga insisted that one of them might have been asked to assist in communion.

I met her in Vancouver in 1983 when she was elected to the Presidium. At first she was ready to refuse her election, as it went against the grain for her to be part of any structure exercising power and authority over others. But it was precisely because of this attitude that the World Council wanted her as a

President. She shared power and opened the way for others, including the poor, the oppressed, and women.

A seasoned lay theologian, she opened up the following text at a WCC Executive meeting, believing that for far too long we had left such passages to the sects. This text was also read at her funeral.

> *On this mountain the Lord of hosts will make for all peoples a feast of rich food, a feast of well-aged wines, of rich food filled with marrow, of well-aged wines strained clear. And he will destroy on this mountain the shroud that is cast over all peoples, the sheet that is spread over all nations; he will swallow up death forever. Then the Lord God will wipe away the tears from all faces, and the disgrace of his people he will take away from all the earth.*
>
> (Isaiah 25.6-8 NRSV)

How singularly appropriate for Marga. The passage contrasts with the previous chapter that speaks of the "ruin of the city" and the downfall of the urban civilization that excluded people from full participation in its life. Sound familiar? Three short verses articulate an alternate vision of the world where God's presence will be recognized through a transformed community. The text uses strong images to communicate hope in a world of despair: a banquet, a veil, and slaying of the monster Leviathan. Marga thought this visionary text had implications for the contemporary ecumenical movement.

"On this mountain" (Mount Zion) is the centre of the new regime God will inaugurate and the site of "a feast of rich food for all the peoples"—a really great party! Marga called it a feast of fat things, rich food filled with marrow, juicy, pithy and filled with vitality. In former days, we used to sing a hymn at Communion that was a foretaste of this joyous gathering celebrating God's presence:

> *This is the hour of banquet and of song; this is the heavenly table spread for me; here let me feast, and feasting, still prolong, the brief bright hour of fellowship with Thee.*

And the poor would be fully present. The wines would be the finest—without dregs or sediment, and well strained. No one would be hungry or thirsty again. It offers the feast as a sign of generosity, security, abundance, and joy.

What a challenging vision this is for the countries of this world, where the rich grow richer, and the poor, poorer. It raises questions about the exclusion of people through the unforgiving market economy; the relentless hunt for new resources and the apparent willingness to do anything to get at them—even at the expense of aboriginal peoples who may own the land. The world appears to be caught in the grip of death, with no power to shake it off.

Marga, who chaired the WCC global conference on "Peace, Justice and the Integrity of Creation," thought the passage had implications for the churches as well. She would have agreed with" former MP Bill Blaikie, who writes about his emerging insights on this matter.

> Arriving at university...I did not yet see that salvation might involve being saved not just from destructive personal behaviour, but also from... oppressive relationships. Nor had I encountered the economy as a moral or theological issue...the prophets were criticizing kings and kingdoms on the basis of how they were treating their people...whether justice was being done. I learned that God takes sides.[1]

Isaiah goes on to say that God will swallow up the veils, webs, shrouds and palls that linger over all the nations. The web of woven lies and the pall that covers relations of nations with nations will be "swallowed up"—that is, destroyed—and truth-telling about the world will emerge. Marga interpreted this to underline the need for a New International Information order.

Currently, news is distorted by the use of euphemisms. Civilian deaths are known as "collateral damage." The greedy free market economy covers the human pain it causes by speaking of unemployment as "downsizing," and higher and high paying jobs as "opportunity." TV advertising projects a product which is always foolproof and within one's grasp financially. There is no room in this scenario for acknowledgement of the growing gap between the rich and the poor. And then there is the world of propaganda, where misleading myths are spun about our country's history, economy, or accomplishments. We continue to embrace the historic mythology that claims North America was "discovered," as though there were no inhabitants living here at the time. One can imagine the indigenous peoples shouting to each other, "We've been discovered!" The text

---

1 Bill Blaikie, *The Bill Blaikie Report: An Insider's Look at Faith and Politics* (Toronto: The United Church of Canada Publishing House, 2011), pp. 50–51.

calls for an end to self-serving propaganda, webs of lies and distortions, empty rhetoric and unfulfilled promises from politicians, the media, or weak-kneed preachers. It calls for the ambiguities in world affairs to be resolved and laid bare. The world is held in the grip of despair and death, and has no will to shake it off. Think slaughter in Syria; genocide in Rwanda; famine in Sudan. This reference to death is not just to "our threescore years and ten," but to all that limits or paralyzes a life, prevents community, diminishes meaning, bends us over, limits our possibilities, invites depression, hosts despair and destroys hope.

The vision then speaks of "God swallowing up death forever." Sounds like Star Wars to me. The poet Isaiah is here attacking the Canaanite myth of Leviathan, the sea monster who represents death—that same monster to whom Milton compares Satan in Book 1 of *Paradise Lost*, and Star Wars draws on when depicting antagonistic dark forces surrounding us. The Hebrew word "swallow" means the same as "destroy." Apparently God will attack this marauding beast Leviathan and will crush and chew it, and we will hear "guzzle, guzzle, munch, munch; gobble, gobble, chomp chomp," just as in John Rutter's musical "Reluctant Dragon." Later, Paul later writes, "Death has been swallowed up in victory" (1 Corinthians 15.54). Marga thought this expressed the conviction and confidence that finally, through God's final victory, there will be an end to apathy, despair, paralysis, and negativity, and we will gain confidence that love is stronger than hate, and life stronger than death.

And then there is that tender line, "God will wipe away the tears," which appears also in Revelation 21.4. Marga knew this meant comfort for the suffering, the lost, the despairing. There will be no need for tears, no sense of loss or deprivation any longer. And God will take away the shame of people, of those who did not have the will or energy to resist "death" and exploitation or conformity, as well of those who allowed poverty and injustice to flourish. Do you count yourself among these?

This vision is not one of "pie in the sky, when you die, by-and-by," but a joyous, noisy, banquet, with the finest food and drink now, in this life. This vision is not one of individualistic morality nor of people praying for the inclusion of all in the future, but a vision of people of all classes, races, and genders eating, drinking, and partying together now, in joyous recognition of their seat at the table God has prepared for them in this time.

To this banquet we all are invited. Do come and enjoy! Marga did.

P. Stephen Burnett, United Kingdom
8 January 1914 – 13 December 1991

Church of England ordained Rev. Canon ('48); Solicitor; Student Christian Movement ('47–'52); Lay Missionary, diocese Sask. Canada ('39–'41); Served in UK Army in India ('44–'45); Vicar of St Mary, Sheffield , UK ('52–'61); Canon of Sheffield Cathedral and Adult Educ. Sec., Diocese of Sheffield, UK ('61–'70); Church of England Board of Adult Education ('70–); Hon. Sec. Fellowship of Maple Leaf ('65–). Married to Joan, two children.

"Why should the churches be left in the hands of conservative people?" asked this tall gangly Englishman of me as we sat chatting in Kensington Gardens in the U.K. He wanted Christians to bring their best thinking and expertise to secular issues in the community, and this required innovative thinking. He had worked in Sheffield, U.K. at a community level for several years, bringing together vocational groups such as Christian lawyers, politicians, and journalists to seek a common path of action on common concerns, such as refugee policy. Later he followed this same pattern nationally as the Director of Adult Education for the Church of England. Now he was urging a similar approach in Canada.

Shortly after I met Stephen Burnett, I read a short article in *Time* magazine about an innovative program a few lay people had launched in Duluth, Minnesota, called "Faith in Life Dialogue." These church folk would identify a movie that dealt with some civic issue, and host an after-movie talk fest to discuss what they had seen. It was a public event, not a church event. I immediately arranged to meet Loren Halverson, a pastor in Minneapolis who was developing this approach to ministry ever since his visit to the Lutheran church in post war Germany. He found the church there still asking two questions: "How could we have known what was going on in our neighbourhood, that Hitler was building gas ovens and exterminating the Jews there?" and "Even if we had known, what could one person do anyway?" So Loren developed his approach in an attempt to answer those two questions. By the time I met him, the program had been developed for Minneapolis and was called Town Meeting. It was essentially an open city wide forum on issues affecting the future of citizens, instigated by churches.

The American Lutherans too, believed that the church's mission was the care of the city, and their concerns dovetailed with those of Anglican Stephen Burnett. Perhaps, with their support, we United Church and ecumenical friends could launch a similar initiative in Canada. We did, and we called it "Town Talk." First Church freed me up to direct the process. John Carrel, Clerk of Session at First Church United, Thunder Bay, Ontario (see p. 138 of this book), wrote me, "Shortly after the last kid stopped being carried to church in a laundry basket, we negotiated a treaty with you. We paid you a stipend to work part time in the congregation, and you were left free to work part time in the community."

Unable to identify the scripture read at Stephen's funeral, I am confident he would have been happy with the following verses, because they express so much the passion and focus of his ministry.

> *The words of the God of Israel: to all the exiles whom I have carried off from Jerusalem to Babylon: Marry wives and beget sons and daughters; take wives for your sons and give your daughters to husbands, so that they may bear sons and daughters and you may increase there and not dwindle away. Seek the welfare of any city to which I have carried you off, and pray to the Lord for it; on its welfare your welfare will depend....when you seek me you shall find me...I will restore your fortunes and gather you again from all the nations...and bring you back to the place from which I carried you into exile.*
>
> (Jeremiah 29.4–7, 13-14 NEB)

What an appropriate text for Stephen Burnett. He believed Christians are called to "the care of the city" where they live. Parish programs limited to church members were not ambitious enough for him. There had to be a focus on community needs and involve ecumenical as well as total community participation.

I knew people had caught on to "Town Talk" when one of my children returned from her Grade 8 class one November, and reported that the teacher had asked the class to write on pollution rather than the usual "How I spent my Summer Holidays." The day before, a TV program had highlighted a documentary on the subject, followed by a radio phone in of viewers' comments. The young people's group at the teacher's church was discussing this topic the next Sunday, based partly on an excellent newspaper article written by a local reporter. Pollution was only one of several burning issues identified by the community of Thunder Bay for public discussion through 1967 Town Talk.

A small ecumenical group of twelve people planned the month long event, which encouraged city-wide talk about the welfare of our city and its 100,000 people. It was an electronic Town meeting that took place simultaneously in every conceivable setting within the month: on radio hotlines; over TV; in regular meetings of local clubs and Boards; in labour unions; schools; university classes; bars; churches; pee wee hockey leagues; libraries; professional groups; sororities; newspapers. Two booklets were distributed by all grocery stores and by every liquor bar in town: one outlining the priority issues identified by the community such as what pollution was caused by flushing one's toilet into the Kam River; the other a theological rationale for the entire program. Sermons were preached on the issues; University convocations invited their honoree to address a Town Talk topic; national expert resource people were hosted by local organizations to speak at their meetings; Libraries mounted special displays of books on Town Talk topics and found the circulation of their books doubled. The daily newspaper published a weekly schedule of events which prompted people to buy the paper to find out what was happening.

The invitation to participate was issued to every conceivable organization listed in the phone book—about 600 of them! We decided on a "blitz" method, whereby for one month, dozens of voluntary groups and also public structures would concentrate on the topics of Town Talk, and suspend their normal routine programs. Organizations would bring both their questions and their resources to the public "Town Jabber" as my mother dubbed it. The main areas the community identified for discussion were 1) Government 2) The city where we lived 3) Education 4) Interpersonal relationships 5) Values and technology 6) Media and communications. If you thought excessive taxation was a burning issue you raised it publicly and waited to see if any allies emerged! The social partnership of mass communications, civic groups, churches and educational institutions meant that when all means of communication were focused simultaneously on a public issue the whole community became excited to talk about the problem together, rather than separately

Although it was given full support by the United Church Presbytery and the ecumenical community, it was not a private event for church members but a public event. The ecumenical community was only the catalyst.

Stephen Burnett helped finance the program through funds from the Fellowship of the Maple Leaf, a forward looking Church of England fund that supported such a public forum for the city. Town Talk addressed the complexity of the modern city and the consequent apathy of citizens by giving people a tool to engage the issues. It addressed two questions, "What is going on in my community?" and "What can I do about it?" One high school principal commented, "I opted out of Town Talk early on because it looked as if the group would be afraid of real controversy. But I opted in half way through, because I saw they were not frightened of it at all. Now I find myself defending the thesis that new life is coming from the churches."

What does the care of the city mean for the faith community today? Has it not always been the calling of Christians to ask the awkward value questions—at the centre of society, not on its private spaces? Not in the sanctuary or individual conscience only, but in the public arena? When I speak publicly about "Religion and Public Policy," I am aware that I could double my audience if I were to conduct a session on meditation. I value meditation, but I also value engagement by the faith community in public policy matters.

I think that the basic role of the churches to ensure that such a public dialogue takes place still remains valid. Our situation is much changed from the sixties, but the calling to find ways in which laity together with clergy must find ways to exercise their vocation of Christian witness on the job, in the marketplace, and in the nation has not changed. Have we retreated from this calling because we are in a survival mode—just keeping a church open?

The believing community—the Church—must always be a source of permanent unrest and disturbance in society, allowing nothing to dissolve or silence it. Constantly our experience of human community (local, national, international) must be subjected to radical critique and reconstruction: for it is only in this way that we can realize and make incarnate the hope and sense of true community that God has promised us. It's really important that you know where the water flushed from your toilet ends up!

Harry F.J. Daniel, India

9 April 1925 – 2 October 1995

Presbyter at St Mark's Cathedral Bangalore, Church of South India ('61–'68); Staff of World Student Christian Federation (early '50s); Gen. Sec. Student Christian Movement of India, Pakistan, Burma, Ceylon; Sec. Urban Industrial Mission (later URM) and East Asia Christian Conference in '70s, concurrently with St Mark's; Staff of World Council of Churches; Associate Gen. Sec. of Christian Conference of Asia ('74–'79); Worked in Hong Kong with Holy Carpenter Church ('79–'83) and with Presbyterian Church, USA both before and after unification; Close colleague of Oh Jae Shik, George Todd and Park Kyung Kyu.; Unorthodox radical Christian. Married to Karin, one daughter Lakshmi, one son Jairaj, grandchildren Zaheu and Shakti.

"The eye of God is watching you," Harry told me in quiet jest at the conclusion of a Greek Orthodox Easter service in Crete in a church adorned with an icon of the eye of God in the ceiling. We were there to participate in the Easter liturgy, including the weekend fast and the break-fast of Easter morning. Etched in my mind was the global gathering of Christians in the town square of Heraklion the previous evening, singing together a traditional hymn of the ecumenical community, "À Toi La Gloire" (VU #173).

It was 1972 and we were at a World Council of Churches consultation on Lay Academies and Related Organizations. Academies were "houses" established in post war Europe in 1945 to take a fresh approach to building bridges between people as many countries struggled with the task of re-building shattered and divided communities. They were centres that created a forum for intellectual, intercultural and ecumenical exchange, rooted in Christian faith but involving people of all faiths and of none. At that time, the WCC gave priority to the ministry of the laity and their secular work in the world, not in the religious institution. I had been invited to share my work on Town Talk, which I have described on pages 17-19 in this book.

The purpose of our gathering at the Orthodox Academy in Crete was to create a worldwide network of people doing similar work. It was my first international church experience outside of Canada, and to say it was a major watershed in my life and understanding of ecumenical ministry would be an understatement. It was my first engagement with Christians from every country around the world, and my first exposure to the Greek Orthodox liturgy for Good Friday and Easter. The gathering was a replay of Pentecost and the difficult word "ecumenism" took on concrete meaning.

Anticipating the beginning of our consultation, we had all assembled outside the meeting place on the top of a high Cretan cliff and suddenly we saw a helicopter landing on a nearby helicopter pad. We were told the Archbishop of Crete had arrived, but there was a lengthy delay. I had not formally met Harry at this point in the proceedings, but he roguishly whispered to me, "He had to pee!" Who on earth was this audacious and slightly vulgar man? It turned out he was also a very serious man. He raised pointed questions about South African apartheid at that Crete meeting although that issue was not on the planned agenda. The organizers were not pleased.

I met Harry many times over the years. On my first visit to the Philippines in 1979, when dictator Marcos was in power, Harry pointed out the bed under which he hastily hidden in 1975 trying to avoid arrest by the state security police because of his work with the poor. But he was arrested, imprisoned for two weeks, and subjected to incessant questioning. He worked in Asia at a time when anyone who worked with the underpaid poor packed into city factories as he did, or criticized the economic system that denied fundamental labor rights to the worker was labeled a Communist, and therefore, one to be eliminated or imprisoned. For him, this was the cost of Christian obedience. For me, who had come from protected middle class Canadian church life, it was a revelation.

His decision after Anglican ordination in the UK was to work ecumenically with students in Geneva, and to continue that work in India. He was committed to working with the poorest, and to humanize industrial structures for all working men and women. His work was not about cultivating friendly relations with Christians of other denominations, nor holding traditional preaching services in the factories, or recruiting new church members. Nor was it social welfare or a relief agency. Rather it was engagement with laity in industry, to try and develop structures that would express dignity for workers and just economic structures. The WCC called this program Urban Rural Mission, a rather awkward name for a movement whose aim was explore new forms of Christian mission in modern society and to identify and act on the need for changes in current economic, social and political practices worldwide. Harry believed that accountability for such a ministry was not to his church, but to his secular colleagues and to the task.

He worked with people who were suffering greatly and for Harry, that meant the presence of Christ in the midst of suffering. Working among the poor in the urban slums of Asian countries, he tried to conscientise labourers and unions to fight for their rights; to influence legislation to afford legal protection to workers re benefits and holidays; to repair community toilets and clear the streets of garbage. His work called forth fierce opposition from the powers-that-be, as poor workers gained more confidence and power to challenge the status quo. He engaged people of all political and faith ideologies about the nature of humanization. Through his work, the church began renewing itself and re discovering the meaning of Jesus Christ in Asia and around the world. That was Harry's splendid unwavering contribution. His wife Karin insisted that the following text be printed on the Order of Service for his funeral, as it was the core meaning of his life.

> *"I have fought the good fight, I have finished the race, I have kept the faith."*
> (2 Timothy 4.7 NRSV)

Harry certainly knew how to fight the good fight, and he never gave any quarter. As early as 1968 Harry insisted that the city would be the place for the new missionary calling. He did not believe in economic security for himself or his family if it meant tying himself to values and practices that in his view denied the gospel. This included not settling down into a respectable parish, such as St Mark's Cathedral in Bangalore, but working to transform the elite of that congregation into a church that reached out to the poor. He seemed to be always short of money for himself, but never hesitated to ask those who had money, to assist in a cause for others in need—such as plane tickets or money for a lawyer to defend a court case. It was never for "charity."

For some time the churches in Canada had a WCC sponsored Urban Rural Mission unit that I chaired. It built on the solid work carried out by Ed File and Stuart Coles. People working on the edges of our society, with down-and-outs, or marginalized folk, gathered once a year to share stories, strategies, successes and failures. It was fully ecumenical and drew community workers from across the country. We developed trust and support for each other, but never did develop an effective strategy for Christians to tackle the problems of city dwellers. We also ran out of money. This work remains unfinished.

There was in Harry's life a seeking of and responsiveness to every new situation, and his ministry always opened up new possibilities for the human community. In his mind, that was what resurrection meant. He insisted that churches on every continent needed to develop new patterns of ministry, authentically indigenous models of ministry, instead of being cookie cutter imitations of each other. Models speak to models in a way that resolutions do not. So, for example, we Canadians can learn from Japanese Christians what it means to be a minority church in a larger non-Christian culture; from China's Protestant post-denominational church what is possible when all Protestant denominations come together in a new church; from poor displaced Roman Catholics in Argentinean "base communities," the nature of hope.

There was also present in Harry's life a confidence that his work with marginalized people was part of God's plan. Not for him future resurrection in some imagined golden cloud. He worked with resurrected communities and hopeful people who know God is to be found with suffering people here, in this world. He fought the authoritarian military and the global economic interests that denied this vision; he never doubted the course he was on and finished it with a flourish; and he kept the faith. Of how many of us can this be said?

James Gareth Endicott, Canada-China
1898 – 1993

Christian missionary, clergyman, socialist; Born in China to a Methodist father who was the second Moderator of the United Church of Canada (1926–28); Founding member of the Student Christian Movement (Victoria College); United Church Missionary in China ('25–46); Initially supported Chiang Kai-shek; Disillusioned with Chiang, and joined forces with the Chinese Communist Party; Resigned from UCC ministry (5 May '46); Continued critique of the Kuomintang government; Chairman Canadian Peace Congress; Senior figure in World Peace Council ('50) which drafted Stockholm Peace Appeal that initiated the "Ban the Bomb" movement; President of the International Institute for Peace ('57–71). Accused USA of biological and chemical warfare in Korean War ('52); Condemned by Canadian politicians and United Church; Awarded Stalin Peace Prize ('52); Broke with Soviet Union ('71); United Church extended formal apology to him ('82). Four children, 13 grandchildren.

In his student days in the early 1920s, this founder of the Student Christian Movement at Victoria College in Toronto sang a rollicking song by fellow SCM'er J.D. Ketchum, which has been passed down through generations of politically and theologically literate students. We sang it with great gusto as students in the SCM in Winnipeg in the 40s, and it is still sung today.

The SCM has found its true vocation
In poisoning the student mind.
Its leaders by astute manipulation
Are poisoning the student mind.
The pious souls are sure that we will go
To toast our toes at furnaces below
If we give heed to leaders who they know
Are poisoning the student mind.

Chorus: Poisoning the student mind. (repeat)
Bad men, bold men, villains double died,
Neath their smiling countenances hide,
Spiritual arsenic and moral cyanide,
For poisoning the student, poisoning the student, poisoning the student mind.

Several verses followed, all seeking to subvert the status quo. The SCM was an ecumenical group on university campuses open to all students who had chosen to become Christian as well as all those who wished to test the claims of that faith. It became known as "the church before the church" and was refreshingly irreverent.

I was taught in Sunday School of the wonderful Christian Chiang Kai-shek and his beautiful wife who were saving China from the pagan Communists. It was widely assumed by Christian churches in Canada that Communism was the enemy. By the time my University days of the forties rolled around, the worm had turned. I became aware that Jim Endicott, a United Church missionary in China, disillusioned after seeing Chiang's officers starve their troops, was denouncing this man and his Nationalist government as corrupt. The scenario heated up when we learned that Endicott had become a strong supporter (but never a member) of the Chinese Communist Party. He began to speak at student demonstrations, urging opposition to the Nationalist government, and provoking criticism from his church. It was fine to applaud his political stance when it was for the status quo, but not acceptable when church members heard him applauding Communism for liberating the poor and starving. He was one of the few who perceived a possible convergence between the Christian church's social gospel movement and Marxian socialism, in pursuit of social justice for all. He was condemned by church and government leaders as well as the media, for supporting the Chinese revolution. When the United Church gave him a warning to either modify his public statements or resign, he resigned from his ministry in the West China Mission on 5 May 1946. Later he made an almost unprecedented move when he also resigned from United Church ministry.

At that time, Canada took its lead in foreign policy from the USA, which was vocally anti-Communist. It was in 1952 when Endicott returned to Canada and publicly charged the USA with using biological and chemical weapons during the Korean War, that all hell broke loose. The United Church, which enjoyed a very high national profile, certainly didn't want to be identified with his stance that contradicted popular and church support of the Chiang Kai-Shek regime. Nor did Canadian politicians. Lester Pearson called Endicott "a Red Stooge," and John Diefenbaker labeled his statements "damnable." Undeterred, he continued his work for peace ("Ban the Bomb") and for the poor and marginalized. He became active internationally in the peace movement and unrepentant, worked for the peaceful co-existence between states with different social systems.

Much later, historical hind sight convinced United Church members of his faithfulness to the gospel in the midst of the long years of hurt and misunderstanding. So it was that I was extraordinarily privileged to be the Moderator of the United Church in 1982, at the General Council meeting in Montreal when a warmly applauded resolution of Council instructed me to deliver its apology to Jim for its critical stance toward him, as well as its mistaken historical policies of the 1950s. He graciously accepted the apology.

Endicott's son Stephen told me the following text was read at his funeral:

Moses was minding the flock of his father-in-law Jethro, priest of Midian. He led the flock along the side of the wilderness and came to Horeb, the mountain of God. There the angel of the Lord appeared to him in the flame of a burning bush. Moses noticed that, although the bush was on fire, it was not being burnt up; so he said to himself, "I must go across to see this wonderful sight. Why does not the bush burn away?" When the Lord saw that Moses had turned aside to look, he called to him out of the bush, "Moses, Moses." And Moses answered, "Yes, I am here." God said, "Come no nearer; take off your sandals; the place where you are standing is holy ground." Then he said, "I am the God of your forefathers, the God of Abraham, the God of Isaac, the God of Jacob," Moses covered his face, for he was afraid to gaze on God. The Lord said, "I have indeed seen the misery of my people in Egypt. I have heard their outcry against their slave-masters. I have taken heed of their sufferings, and have come down to rescue them from the power of Egypt, and to bring them up out of that country into a fine, broad land; it is a land flowing with milk and honey....the outcry of the Israelites has now reached me; yes...I will send you to Pharaoh and you shall bring my people Israel out of Egypt." (Exodus 3:1-10 NEB)

What an appropriate text to express Endicott's work among the poor in China. It took the United Church so long before recognizing his prophetic leadership. He burst through conventional categories, disregarded the pedigree of people, crossed artificial boundaries and worked with whoever was seeking economic justice for the poor. This man took part in the major struggles of the 20th century: social justice, national liberation of China, and world peace. He continued his work for the dispossessed until his death.

The text implies oppressive situations with which we are all familiar: rat race jobs; ageism discrimination; no job prospects; temporary migrant workers ;distorted family relationships; loss of meaning; mental health problems, depression. Many indigenous peoples of Canada are caught in the downward spiral of social welfare. Many in the churches do not to speak up against these inequities. Some do.

What an appropriate text for us who have been called out of a world filled with greed, self-sufficiency, consumerism, and anxiety, to embrace obedience, generosity, interdependence; self-giving and trust. Here is a text that speaks to fear and hopelessness.

Mind you, it's not everyone sees this very active liberating God creating new possibilities for our lives and for the world. Have you read this poem by Elizabeth Barrett Browning?

Earth's crammed with heaven, and every bush aflame with God.
But only those who see, take off their shoes. The rest?
They sit around and eat blackberries.

Eating blackberries was not for Jim Endicott.

Alice Mildred (Boomhour) Heap, Canada

20 July 1925 – 24 March 2012

Christian Socialist; Community activist; feminist; pacifist; Student Christian Movement ('45); Member of an Anglican Religious Order-Society of the Catholic Commonwealth (Marxist Anglicans); Attended founding of Canadian Peace Congress ('48); Church Peace Mission and Easter Peace Marches (60s); Member of Communications Energy and Paper workers union; active in NDP (socialist caucus delegate); Practiced radical hospitality with war resisters, civil rights activists, farm workers. Married to Dan, seven children, 18 grandchildren, two great-grandchildren.

There was no mistaking the meaning of her life. No "Abide with Me" or "Shall We Gather at the River" for her. Everyone at Alice Heap's funeral sang "Bread and Roses," that wonderful song that women factory workers in the USA sang so many years ago to protest horrific working conditions and starvation wages, and which many still sing today.

> *As we go marching, marching, unnumbered women dead*
> *Go crying through our singing their ancient call for bread.*
> *Small art and love and beauty their drudging spirits knew,*
> *Yes it is bread we fight for, but we fight for roses too.*

I met Alice after she had married Dan, as we were members of the Canadian SCM in the late forties. Later, we became aware of her practical and extreme Christian solidarity and her faith at work when she was awarded the Bishop's Award for Faithful Service in 2000 for her work at Holy Trinity church in social housing, support group for released offenders, and anti-poverty work. She worked with the Canadian Council for Refugees as well as the Christian Peacemaker Teams—always with people at the bottom of the rung.

The following scripture texts were printed on the calendar of Alice's funeral, and were also used for morning and evening prayers and for the installation of new members, by the Society of the Catholic Commonwealth, to which she belonged. Both are singularly appropriate for her consistently radical approach to life.

> *The work of Justice shall be peace, and the effect of Justice quietness and confidence forever.*
>
> (Isaiah 32.17 adapted from KJV)

> *Keep ye Judgment, and do Justice: for my Salvation is near to come and my Justice to be revealed.*
>
> (Isaiah 56.1 adapted from KJV)

What loaded words! Justice, peace, salvation. And how appropriate to honour Alice, whose life was so given to people through the justice and peace movements. She practiced radical hospitality all her life. She opened her home to SCM work campers, war resisters, civil rights activist, farm workers, or whoever needed a bed that particular night. She took part in SCM student-in-industry summer work camps, worked in factories, and joined with Quebec trade unionist Madeleine Parent in organizing workers. For her, that was the work the gospel required.

And how appropriate for those of us living in a conflicted and war torn world. Indeed the 10th Assembly of the World Council of Churches in Bussan, Korea in 1213 had as its theme, "God of life, lead us to justice and peace."

Let's look at this very strong poetry of Isaiah. These passages will mean much more for to us if we look at the key words that are not separate, but part of the whole. Parallelism is a chief characteristic of Hebrew poetry. Key words such as peace, justice, righteousness, and salvation are not separate but belong to the whole passage. They are meant to have a somewhat cumulative interactive effect on the reader. I am indebted to the Rev. Dr. Philip Potter, former General Secretary of the World Council of Churches, for the insights into these words.

Justice is sometimes translated as "deliverance," or more usually as "righteousness." It means integrity of being, which enables one to give the other person their due. In Arabic, when a date is just ripe it is "righteous." So a person is righteous when she is just what a human being ought to be. The Hebrew word *sevek* means a human being is fully himself when righteous, recognizing the rights of the other. So the Jewish community honoured some who had helped Jews escape the Holocaust with the term "righteous Gentiles."

"The work of justice shall be peace." When I lived in Hamilton I would frequently phone my colleagues at the Jewish Centre down the street, and be greeted by that gracious word *shalom*. I always felt slightly like a barbarian by responding "hello." Shalom is a greeting in a relationship that conveys strength through sharing. It is the opposite of a torn piece of cloth; it is wholeness. To "go in peace" means you are freed of all that kept you from being a full human being into a life of self-giving, and strong enough to not hold back The totality of this is contained in the word *shalom*.

Then there is the word salvation. The Hebrew word for salvation means "wide, spacious, liberated, free." What an appropriate meaning that developed out of a people who were frequently pushed into a corner and confined. There is no division between material and spiritual. God "saves" because God is the truly fee, liberated, reliable one.

The Greek word meaning "save," "salvation," or "saviour" were all taken from the secular and religious language of the Greco-Roman world. In Greek literature those words described deliverance from death; from perils of the sea; from imprisonment of the body; and for immortality from death. The philosophers used the term to mean liberation from ignorance, false opinion, or superstition.

The Latin *salus* has been adapted by the French as "salut." It is the root of the English word "salvation." It means authenticity, integrity of being, liberated from oneself, the state of being sound.

So all of that is implied in the two short verses Alice had printed on the front of her funeral bulletin! But just in case we had missed the point, as we individually came forward to place sand on her ashes as the service came to a conclusion, we sang,

When We Make Peace instead of War
(to the tune of "When the Saints Go Marching In" adapted by the Raging Grannies)

When we make peace, instead of war (Repeat)
Oh I want to be in that number
When we make peace instead of war.

When there's respect for worker's rights (Repeat)
Oh I want to be in that number
When there's respect for worker's rights.

When there's respect for human rights (Repeat)
Oh I want to be in that number,
When there's respect for human rights.

When justice rules, instead of force (Repeat)
Oh I want to be in that number
When justice rules instead of force.

So the implications for the faith community are clear. Is not the mark of a Christian to share the suffering of the people and God's suffering in the world and not necessarily more Bible reading or more church attendance? Is it not to develop a life posture of justice for those who have never received their due? I think in that lies our salvation. And Alice led the way.

KIM DAE-JUNG, SOUTH KOREA (ROK)

3 December 1925 – 18 August 2009

Nobel Peace Prize, ('01); Advocate for democracy, human rights, reunification of Korean peninsula; Baptized Roman Catholic ('57); Politician-elected to National Assembly ('61); Presidential candidate of New Democratic Party ('71); Abducted by Korean CIA in Tokyo and placed under house arrest ('73); Survived five attempts on his life; as leader of pro-democracy movement in South Korea joined in issuing "Independence Day Declaration for Democratization" ('76); Native of Kwangju province, site of infamous massacre May, ('80); Political prisoner charged with treason ('80) and sentenced to death; sentence commuted to life imprisonment; exiled to USA ('82); Returned to Korea ('85); elected President ('97–'03); Joint declaration with North Korea for engagement 15 June 2000; Given a State funeral 18 Aug. 2009. Married to Lee Hee-Ho.

It was at a secret and illegal clandestine meeting of relatives of political prisoners organized by Korean churches in 1981 that I met Lee Hee-Ho. She told me about her husband Kim Dae-Jung, a Presidential candidate, who was then in prison for his pro-democracy actions in a country under authoritarian rule and martial law. She gave me a Korean handcrafted cord necklace which I continue to wear and treasure.

I met this remarkable man twice. The first time was in Ottawa when I was a Senator, and he recalled the resolution by the Canadian Parliament supporting the intervention of the USA, asking for clemency to repeal the death sentence given to him in 1980 by the dictator Chun Doo Hwan His courageous work for democracy had made him an international celebrity, and international pressure saved his life. Later, in Seoul, South Korea, I met him again when as President he invited representatives from countries that had supported him throughout the years of struggle for democracy in his country. Former Moderator Lee Sang Chul and I were invited from Canada. On this occasion, people from many countries were seated around tables of eight to receive the then President, who had with him a briefing book containing our names and affiliations. When he came to my table, he looked at me and said, "You weren't a Senator when you were here about Kwangju." "No, I responded, nor were you President. You were in prison." We both laughed.

The reference to Kwangju, near Kim's home, was to the 18 May 1980 pro-democracy demonstration when so many students were massacred and Kim Dae-Jung himself was arrested on orders of the then dictator Chun Doo-hwan. In 1997 he was pardoned for his crimes by the then President Dae-Jung.

One cannot readily summarize this man's life. It was a mixture of vision, failure, danger, persistence and accomplishment. His vision, embraced by many Koreans, was reconciliation, reunification, and democratization of the two Koreas, sadly divided in 1950 by the politics of the post war world. His failure was to lose four election attempts at President. He encountered danger because of his pro-democracy stance, and endured ten years of house arrest, six years in prison, a kidnapping, an exile, an "intentional" car accident, a rigged trial and a sentence of death. His persistence showed in his lifelong struggle against authoritarian rule in Korea. His accomplishments are legion. The Nobel Peace Prize was given to him for his leadership of millions of Koreans in securing democracy and an economically viable state. He convened the ground breaking Inter-Korean Summit of June 2000 between the two Koreas that had been divided for 55 years, and enunciated his "Sunshine Policy." His faith shone when as President in 1997, having won the first democratic election of Korea, he publicly forgave two former dictators for their crimes against their own people.

When I enquired about the scripture read at the funeral of this faithful Roman Catholic, I received the following message, courtesy of Lee Moon-Sook, and Mary Collins, a United Church fraternal worker with the Presbyterian Church of the Republic of Korea (South Korea).

"For a state funeral, leaders representing different religions offer prayers and that is all that religious communities are supposed to do in these services. Scripture reading was not done. At the Seoul National Cemetery there was another ritual where Lee Hae-Dong prayed so I asked him if there had been a Bible reading. He says he just cited John 11.25-26 in his prayer during the service at the Cemetery."

> *Jesus said to her, "I am the resurrection and the life. Those who believe in me, even though they die, will live, and everyone who lives and believes in me will never die. Do you believe this?"* (John 11.25–26 NRSV)

What does this mean? Surely not the resuscitation of a corpse. Surely a confirmation of the continuing strength of the love and justice that was part of this person's life and witness. Life and love keep popping up in people's lives, even in situations of utter depravity and hopelessness. Is the Biblical narrative not saying that continuity and strength of love and justice are built into the life of humans and the earth itself? Is it not affirming that a just and compassionate life confirms the Easter structure of human existence? Hopelessness and despair can apparently be transformed into indignation and courage. Abandonment at the very moment of death can become the certainty of God's presence. Resurrection (which means "to stand up for") is part of that certainty.

I keep meeting resurrected people and resurrected communities. One such is Anglican priest Michael Lapsley, who worked as an anti-apartheid activist during the South African apartheid years. He received and opened a parcel bomb at his home. It exploded and he lost his arms from the elbows down and sight in one eye. Many friends visited him in the hospital to sympathize and tell him all the things he would no longer be able to do. Finally, one person came in and said to him, "Michael, you are now eminently equipped to start a movement for reconciliation between people who are enemies." Michael has spent the rest of his life doing just that through his Institute for the Healing of Memories, and establishing a community of the resurrection. The last time I saw him he was wondering if he could be useful in assisting in the reconciliation process between the "settler society" and the indigenous peoples in Canada.

Dorothee Sölle writes about her five-year-old granddaughter who came home from kindergarten and said, "What happened to Jesus was very bad; they made him dead with nails through his hands. But then, there was Easter and, ha-ha, he got up again."²

The Greek word "stand" shares the same root as "resurrection." We need to stand up to our churches and governments on issues that oppress or alienate the poor and dispossessed. That is one expression of resurrection, and the hope for a fresh national life and a new governance for which the Hebrew prophets longed.

The life of Kim Dae-Jung was filled with risk, death and failure, followed by new beginnings, resurrections, and hope. He "stood up" for what he believed, and inspired a generation of Koreans to create a community that stood up for democracy in their country. Perhaps one contribution Canadian churches can make to the body politic is to work to restore credibility to our political process and institutions. It will not be without struggle and long term commitment.

---

2   Dorothee Sölle, *Against the Wind: Memoir of a Radical Christian.* Trans. Barbara and Martin Rumscheidt (Minneapolis, MN: Augsburg Fortress Press, 1999), p.154.

GARTH WARREN LEGGE, CANADA

25 July 1922 – 21 February 2007

Minister of United Church of Canada; Served pastorates in northern Quebec and Ontario ('52–'59); Missionary in Northern Rhodesia (now Zambia) and Moderator of the United Church of Central Africa ('59–'64); Staff in Division of World Outreach ('65–'77) and its General Sec. ('77–'87); Acting Gen. Sec. of Canadian Council of Churches; Monitor of South Africa Elections post-apartheid ('94). Married to Joyce, three children, four grandchildren.

"God smiles as Garth reaches the doorstep of heaven. 'Well done Garth. Come on in and refresh yourself,' God says. In the time it takes for God to turn around, Garth will have organized a group of angels for international solidarity." These words spoken by Pierre Goldberger at Garth's funeral are a fitting image of the man we honour. Pierre was a United Church minister who worked closely with Garth in implementing actions of solidarity with the ecumenical partners of the United Church in the Global south. Garth received his name after his mother had read a story during her pregnancy in which the hero was called Garth. It means "full of life and energy with a few weeds thrown in."

His greatest gift to the ecumenical community and church was his time with the Division of World Outreach with its primary focus on global and ecumenical relationships of the United Church worldwide. It was the time of the Dual Mandate: Doing Mission = Doing Justice. This policy brought the personal and political together. He joined the United Church of Zambia in fighting for the independence of that country, practiced solidarity with South African churches working to end apartheid, and supported the United Church's work with partners that shared this vision globally. This was a watershed in terms of the church's understanding of mission, as it entered into authentic partnerships with indigenous churches around the globe. His work in the 60s divesting Canadian companies of economic control in Trinidad, his subsequent work against Canadian companies investing in apartheid South Africa, as well as his monitoring of that country's 1994 elections led to his being awarded the Order of Canada. Garth's charisma of humility enabled him to listen to the voices of the Two Thirds World.

Consistently he would rise to his feet at the Executive meeting of the General Council of the United Church, and move a motion to equalize salaries of all its ministers, believing in the parity of ministers. He believed that whether one was serving as minister in a large Toronto congregation with all its extra perks, or as a missionary in India, on minimum salary without any perks, salaries should be the same. Just as consistently, the Executive voted him down.

A text read at his funeral was as follows:

> *When he came to Nazareth where he had been brought up, he went to the synagogue on the sabbath day, as was his custom. He stood up to read, and the scroll of the prophet Isaiah was given to him. He unrolled the scroll and found the place where it was written, "The Spirit of the Lord is upon me, because he has anointed me to bring good news to the poor. He has sent me to proclaim release to the captives and recovery of sight to the blind, to let the oppressed go free, to proclaim the year of the Lord's favour." And he rolled up the scroll, gave it back to the attendant, and sat down. The eyes of all in the synagogue were fixed on him. Then he began to say to them, "Today this scripture has been fulfilled in your hearing."* (Luke 4.16–21 NRSV)

This passage announces the beginning of Jesus public ministry. At first "they all spoke well of him." Was he not Joseph's son? For many, the passage called to mind Isaiah 61 with its similar promise of the coming reversal of the fortunes of Israel. The "year of the Lord's favour" referred to the visionary "Year of Jubilee" outlined in Leviticus 25, in which land taken from the poor was restored to its owner, debts were forgiven, and slaves were to be freed. No wonder they all spoke well of him. A new day was dawning at last.

But then he began to tell them what was involved in his radical vision of the re-ordered community. He told them about Elijah's ministry to a foreigner—a widow in Sidon, and of Elisha's cleansing of a foreigner, Naaman the Syrian. Was he suggesting that God's mercy and justice extends far beyond the small group of people in Nazareth? Was he announcing that all the benefits of the Year of Jubilee were also for foreigners and for the disadvantaged? Was he suggesting a re-ordering of social relationships between the advantaged and the down-and-outs, the prisoners, the oppressed? This statement of care for the outsiders and foreigners and "good news to the poor"—a deep hope for the reordering of the economics of the community—provoked those who benefited from the status quo. No wonder they reacted with hostility.

> *All in the synagogue ... were filled with wrath ... put him out of the city, and led him to the brow of the hill ... that they might throw him down headlong.*
> (Luke 4.28–29 RSV)

This passage that gives the clue to Jesus' entire ministry did not sit well with the folk in Nazareth, just as it does not sit well with folk today who are content with the status quo, be it religious or economic.

This passage is so appropriate for Garth Legge and reflects his lifelong passion for justice and right relationships between people. His Christian faith was steeped in social analysis, biblically informed, praxis oriented and globally applicable. He brought his best thinking to his practice of mission. He understood partnership as reciprocal. Gone was the patronizing colonial concept of mission. Gone was the domination of northern churches (with money) over southern churches (without money.) The sharing of resources by northern churches was matched by southern churches with gifts of insight, creative patterns of ministry, and a gentle critique of North American cultural practices, sometimes supported by northern faith communities.

So often we so spiritualize this passage that it loses its bite. In response to the question what does "good news to the poor mean?" some might say "salvation." But such an answer would not provoke hostility against the one who makes the announcement. It must have implied economic changes. The invocation of "the Year of the Lord's favour" or "the acceptable year of the Lord"

(RSV), as mentioned above, was clearly a reference to the "Year of Jubilee." which meant a re-ordering of economic relationships. No wonder the people of Nazareth were ready to kill Jesus for threatening their privileged way of life with his talk of "good news to the poor."

"Release to the prisoners" (NEB) was the second announcement. I was recently at a lecture by Sister Prejean, the Catholic nun who accompanies men on Death Row in the USA to their execution. After she had given us a passionate and clear account of her ministry to these men, someone at the back of the room raised his hand for a question. "Since none of us will ever see the inside of a prison," he said, "could you tell us what it is like?" She responded quickly and sharply, "Why won't you ever see the inside of a prison? Have you never read the gospel's admonition to bring release to the prisoners?" Dead silence descended on the room.

Canada is building more and bigger prisons. Aboriginal youth make up a disproportionate percentage of the prisoners. The John Howard Society or the Elizabeth Fry Society assist former prisoners in their re-entry into society. The Friends of Dismas (the name of the repentant thief at the time of Jesus' crucifixion) is an ecumenical ministry that encourages a commitment to walk on a one-to-one basis with an ex-prisoner during that difficult time of readjustment to society. It is a ministry of friendship, prayer and support for people after a long period of incarceration. It welcomes volunteers, and sponsors an annual Restorative Justice Conference. What is your church's ministry to prisoners?

"Recovery of sight to the blind." In 1973 in Hamilton, three refugees from Chile told me about the disastrous coup in Chile, the overthrow of the socialist government, the ascension of the dictator Pinochet, the complicity of the Americans, and the consequent oppression in the country. I had been living in a North American bubble. Now I began to see the world with entirely new eyes.

"Let the oppressed go free." Here the essence of the gospel is announced as enabling every person to escape from whatever prevents them from becoming an authentic human being in the eyes of God. Those who keep others in "captivity," whether economic, political, or social, will oppose any efforts to open up new vistas for people bound to accepted roles. Conflict and challenge lie ahead for those of us who side with the oppressed, which Garth Legge knew well.

C.F. BYERS NAUDÉ, SOUTH AFRICA
10 May 1915 – 7 September 2004

Anti-apartheid activist and reconciler; Entrenched religious Afrikaner nationalist background; Clergyman of Dutch Reformed Church, and for 23 years and until 1960 a member of Broederbond, a closed society of Afrikaner leaders who supported apartheid; Later, a founder of ecumenical anti-apartheid, multi-racial Christian Institute ('61); Resigned as Moderator of Dutch Reformed Church Synod, Southern Transvaal ('63); Stripped of his status as minister ('63); Resigned from Broederbond; together with 18 black organizations, staff of the Christian Institute were banned for eight years ('77–'85); Ordained into African Reformed Church ('88–'85); Welcomed back into Dutch Reformed church ('94); Gen. Sec. of South African Council of Churches ('85–'87). Married to Ilse, three sons, one daughter, four grandchildren, four great-grandchildren.

"The secret police have us under surveillance," he said. "They are very efficient, but they won't see my sleight of hand." The day I left the country, when Naudé saw me off at the airport, he surreptitiously slipped a bulky letter under my coat He then told me he had stayed up all night typing out the theological rationale for regarding apartheid in South Africa as a heresy. "Heresy is not doctrine." he told me. "It is actions." He directed me to deliver his manuscript to James McCord, President of the World Alliance of Reformed Churches meeting in Ottawa, when I returned to Canada in two days time. I did so, noting that in an act of solidarity, black delegates at that meeting refused to participate in communion with the white delegates in Canada, since this was forbidden in South Africa. The next day a resolution was passed declaring that the theological justification for apartheid was a heresy, and suspending from membership two white South African churches. Later one was reinstated after acknowledging apartheid as a heresy. Thus Naudé's document confirmed, consolidated, and strengthened opposition to apartheid by Reformed congregations around the world.

At the time, the United Church's strong public opposition to apartheid, along with others in the World Council of Churches, called forth the full wrath of the South African Government. Wishing to visit and lend the solidarity of the United Church to the anti-apartheid movement, I knew that if I applied for entry into South Africa as Moderator of the church (which I was at the time), I would be denied entry. So I applied as "tourist, housewife" (which I also was!). I phoned Primate Ted Scott of the Anglican Church, who, through his connections with Canada's Foreign Affairs staff, pulled the strings and I got my visa.

Naudé was playing a crucial role in supporting the liberation struggle for blacks in his country when I met him in 1982. He had become one of the most respected stalwarts of South Africa's liberation struggle. At the time, he was banned for refusing to testify before the Parliamentary Commission investigating the Christian Institute, a multiracial interdenominational Christian organization fighting for those who had no political or legal rights. "If laws are immoral," he told me, "Christians must resist." Banning meant he could talk to only one person at a time. His wife retired to the kitchen and we talked in his living room. When asked to preach he always accepted, explaining to the state police that he was addressing his remarks to only one person in the congregation, and he couldn't help it if others listened in. Talk about courage!

He had been a member of the exclusive Afrikaner Broederbond (of which his father was a founding member) for years. When he left the organization at age forty-five in 1960, he was shunned and vilified by both family and religious colleagues. He had joined "the enemy." Only years later (1994) was he welcomed back into the Dutch Reformed Church, when the tide of the struggle started to turn, thus advancing the spirit of reconciliation that was a mark of his remarkable life and witness. When I asked Naudé how his radical change from apartheid supporter to anti-apartheid activist came about, he replied, "I read the gospels!" Two other events consolidated his conversion. In his position as moderator, young white ministers exposed him to the devastating experiences in their black congregations where he found families deeply divided because of the Mixed Marriages Act or the Group Areas Act. He was deeply troubled. Then came Sharpeville in 1960 when a peaceful protest was disrupted by sixty-nine black people being shot in the back by Government troops He made his decision.

He became one of the closest allies of the black community through his work at the Christian Institute. Just how close is illustrated by this excerpt from a poem "Oom Bey Nine Nine," written and read at Naudé's funeral by Noko (Johannes) Choshi, a Security officer at Elm Park Retirement Village, and sent to me by Liesel, Byer's daughter: "Who is he? He is a comrade, nine nine; He is a Hero, nine nine; He ran the race and won it, nine nine; he fought for change, nine nine; He fought for freedom, nine nine."[3]

The following text, quoted by Nelson Mandela on the 80th birthday of Byers Naudé in 1995, probably best sums up the essence of the man.

> *By faith Moses, when he was grown up, refused to be called a son of Pharaoh's daughter, choosing rather to share ill-treatment with the people of God than to enjoy the fleeting pleasures of sin. He considered abuse suffered for the Christ to be greater wealth than the treasures of Egypt, for he was looking ahead to the reward. By faith he left Egypt, unafraid of the king's anger; for he persevered, as though he saw him who is invisible.* (Hebrews 11.24–27 NRSV)

Naudé rejected his privileged birth position as a white man, threw in his lot with the exploited black gold miners and their female "nanny" counterparts, and paid the price. He rejected race and class as the definitive criteria for acceptance of citizenship, and worked rather for inclusion of all. The text lifts him up as a living spirit of hope for racial justice and reconciliation.

And what does passage mean for our faith community? Is not one implication the necessity of recognizing and acknowledging our own privileged position as middle or upper class whites in Canada? Why is it the United Church seldom focuses on class divisions? Bill Blaikie, a United Church minister and also former MP and Speaker of the House, is not shy about speaking on this issue. He laments that Canadians are loathe to look seriously at economic injustices and the need for fundamental structural change in the economic system we embrace. Author Chris Hedges claimed in a Jan. 2013 article in the *United Church Observer* that "the white liberal church walked out on Martin Luther King's call for economic justice. Racial justice...was fine, but challenging systems of economic

---

3 "Nine nine" means "for sure" in township slang.

power was something that made them very uncomfortable."

The Biblical text also testifies to the necessity of resistance to that which contradicts the very essence of Christian faith. Robust spirituality is always exhibited by acts of resistance to that which degrades or oppresses, followed by justice and reconciliation.

Dorothee Sölle was a German feminist theologian who knew all about resistance during the Nazi era.[4] Here are excerpts from her conversation with Beyers Naudé in 1968:

> There is a deeply grounded wrong understanding of God's intention with us, in the understanding of salvation as salvation of individuals who will be freed from this more or less bad world which never can be changed. It's not an understanding of the kingdom of God, it's about salvation of the ego in a way, so individualism is really at the heart of this form of religion...I have tried to do a theology of liberation for first world citizens in my own country....How should we, where do we invest our money, for example?... so "the earth is the Lord's" means the earth is not General Motors, not the united Food Companies, or whoever you could mention of those who own the earth....It is not the Pentagon's....That means, of course, that you get ostracized; you get into trouble with family and friends, and many other people, and the media, etc., etc. They just make you into a non-person... God's work...starts...with the poor...and listening to the poor gives you enormous strength.[5]

What about Canadian Christians? There are still lots of silences or conflict, when the church critiques the oil sands in Alberta, or questionable labour policies and practices of Canadian mining companies in the Congo. And more silence, when it highlights the precarious situation of Filipino nannies in Canada, heavily dependent on the goodwill of their employer or the efficacy of the Indian Act and the intolerable situation of aboriginal peoples in this country of ours.

What situations of profound injustice exist in your community, your country? Do you remain silent? Where do you stand on these issues?

---
4 See the entry on Dorothee Sölle on page 82 of this book.
5 Dorothee Sölle and C.F. Byers Naudé, *Hope for Faith: A Conversation* (Geneva: WCC Publications / Grand Rapids, MI: Wm. B. Eerdmans, 1986), pp. 13-25, 34.

OH JAE SHIK, SOUTH KOREA (ROK)
15 December 1932 – 3 January 2013

Community organizer in Asia; Ecumenist; Passionate human rights and peace activist; Student Christian Movement ('60–'64); Yale Divinity School and Urban Rural Mission training with Saul Alinsky ('66); Unified YMCA and SCM into Korean Student Christian Federation ('67–68); Succeeded Harry Daniel as Sec. Urban Rural Mission ('70); Sec. of Christian Conference of Asia Urban Rural Mission ('70–'81); Assoc. Gen. Sec. of Korean National Council of Churches ('82–'88), which launched Korean Reunification and forged the Declaration of Korean Churches for Reunification of the Korean People; Director of World Council of Churches Participation in Development ('88–'93); Director Social Education of Korean Christian Academy ('94–'06); Founded Participation Solidarity, the largest and most influential NGO in South Korea ('94–'96); World Vision-Asia including North Korea development work ('97–'02): Director of International Department of Aid to North Korea ('98–'02); Pres. Advisory Committee on National Reunification ('98–'02); Married to Noh Shin, two daughters, one son.

The first time I met Oh Jae Shik was in the late 70s at a European WCC meeting on Human Rights. In the midst of the meeting, suddenly Jae Shik stood up and hurried off to hide himself in a nearby closet. Almost immediately two uniformed Koreans appeared and asked if we knew Jae Shik's whereabouts. Of course we all said no. That was my introduction to the perils of opposing the then dictatorship in Korea.

Jae Shik's early exposure to the Student Christian Movement and his training with Saul Alinsky in the USA were foundational in his practice of community organizing with the poor. Alinksy required his trainees to venture into the streets for two weeks, give someone a $10 bill, and wait for a reaction. Jae Shik discovered some recipients were humiliated, some insulted, some provoked to slap him, and women refusing to "be bought." If charity was not the way, then what was? How could people gain control over their own future, both economically and politically and have justice replace charity?

Several events galvanized Jae Shik into a life commitment to community organizing for better housing, a living wage, and safety in the workplace, mainly through Urban Rural Mission of the churches. There was his early training and his understanding of Christian faith as having to do with liberation, justice and authenticity for human beings and community. But there was more. An Asian man called Tae had burnt himself to death to protest poor working conditions. There was the Kwangju uprising in Korea on 18 May 1980 in order to establish democracy, freedom and human rights in the face of a brutal military regime that mistakenly spoke of this uprising as "a rebellion backed by seditious communists." He became the backbone of community organizing in Asia (1971–93), working ecumenically in the Philippines, Korea, India, Sri Lanka and Myanmar as well as at a Geneva base with the World Council of Churches. His commitment to human rights led him to support pro-democracy movements in Asia. This got him into serious problems with authoritarian regimes such as Korea and the Philippines when they imposed martial law on their citizens. Yet I never met the man but he had a smile on his face.

His pro-democracy posture led to his work for peace and reunification on the Korean peninsula, and when he had the opportunity with World Vision of working in North Korea, he did so, visiting it 16 times between 1997 and 2003. His work then became not only advocacy for reunification of the two Koreas, but introducing virus free seed potato tubes and making agricultural development project proposals in that famine struck vilified country.

His funeral underlined the wide scope of his relationships. A Buddhist monk read a poem; the former Moderator of the National Council of Churches in Japan spoke; a Filipino song was sung; and this scripture was read by and Indonesian student of the Hanshin University Ecumenical Studies in Social Transformation Department:

> *Then Moses went up from the lowlands of Moab to Mount Nebo, to the top of Pisgah, eastwards from Jericho, and the Lord showed him the whole land: Gilead as far as Dan; the whole of Naphtali; the territory of Ephriam and Manesseh, and all Judah as far as the western sea; the Negeb and the plain; the valley of Jericho, the Vale of Palm Trees, as far as Zoar. The Lord said to him, "This is the land which I swore to Abraham, Isaac and Jacob that I would give to their descendants. I have let you see it with your own eyes, but you shall not cross over into it." There in the land of Moab Moses the servant of the Lord died, as the Lord had said. He was buried in a valley in Moab opposite Beth-peor, but to this day no one knows his burial-place.* (Deuteronomy 34.1–6 NEB)

How appropriate for this leader Oh Jae Shik, who saw the vision of a new landscape so clearly, primarily the reunification of North and South Korea, but died before he saw his vision fulfilled. Although he worked tirelessly for human rights and humane working conditions in all of the Asian countries, he didn't live to see it come about.

I last saw Jae Shik in 2002 in Seoul, South Korea, when some of those who had partnered with us in the United Church of Canada in our joint successful struggle to establish democracy in South Korea hosted a small dinner to celebrate our lifelong commitments and fellowship. Lee Sang Chul, former Moderator of our church, was present; so was Park Kyung-Kyu, a staunch ally in the struggle after the Kwangju massacre; and Kang Moon-Kyu, another reliable ally. Jae Shik was still smiling. In 2011 he wrote me on the death of one our prized colleagues, Rhea Whitehead (see p. 128 of this book).

> Our association was intense and long. For me, our friendship as collaboration was and is an on-going life-together. I have not and would not house it as memories of the past. Lois and Rhea of Canada, Peggy and Pat of New York, just to name a few, were pillars of our struggle as well as life. For almost two decades of our struggle for human rights, democracy and peace we could not have maintained our steadfast stance without having solidarity support of ecumenical friends. I personally think that our solidarity was more than a support. It was a shared life, confessing and praying together. We were led into a common vision, life and action. My life design before joining the struggle was different from where I ended up. I would follow your speculation to say, "I suspect the Holy Spirit was in there as well!" For me it was and has been a life

together that is still to continue till the end of mine.

And I expect he is still smiling.

"For me, it has been a life together." Many say the ecumenical movement has lost its energy. Formal merger of churches is no longer on the agenda. How will "life together" be expressed? For some time the divisions within Christendom have not been denominational, but between those who understand Christian faith as private and individualistic and those who practice it as communal and with public implications; between those who judge "success" by numbers of members and those who look to be the small "salty" group who lend flavour and zest to a given society.

The meaning of the Greek word *oikoumene* ("ecumenical") means "the whole inhabited world." God so loved the world and is hard at work in the world through the Holy Spirit. So just as Jae Shik worked for the common good with Buddhists, Indonesians, Koreans, Japanese, even people in the authoritarian regime in North Korea, so our churches need to working for the common good with the rich assortment of faiths, nationalities, and economic classes in Canada. Our questions need to be, "What does my faith and my faith community bring to the common good where I live?" "Where is the possibility of life together?" Rather than the question I hear so frequently, "How can we keep the doors of our church open?"

At a prayer gathering for Jae Shik at the funeral home prior to the official service, this text was read:

> *Grace to you and peace from God the Father and the Lord Jesus Christ. Our thanks are always due to God for you, brothers. It is right that we should thank him, because your faith increases mightily, and the love you have, each for all and all for each, grows even greater. Indeed we boast about you ourselves among the congregations of God's people, because your faith remains so steadfast under all your persecutions, and all the troubles you endure.*
>
> (2 Thessalonians 1.2–4 NEB)

"All persecutions and troubles" of the victims of human rights abuses included harassment, intimidation, imprisonment, torture, betrayal, and death. But despite these costs, this gentle, formidable smiling giant persisted in his faithfulness to affirm the sacredness of human beings, and endured persecution for his continued advocacy with, not for, the poor. And so we boast of him.

MARIA TERESA PORCILE SANTISO, URUGUAY

1943 – 18 June 2001

Uruguayan Roman Catholic lay theologian; Feminist; Ecumenist; Dr. of Theology (University of Fribourg, Switzerland); Prof. of Philosophy (University of Montevideo, Uruguay); Member Pontifical Council for Promoting Christian Unity, Vatican; Only woman admitted to Assembly of Latin American Bishops, Puebla; Speaker at UN World Conference of Women, Bejing ('85); Contributor to the World Council of Churches' Sheffield Conference on Men and Women in Church and Society ('81); Participant in WCC Faith and Order Commission in Lima, Peru ('82); Observer at WCC 6th Assembly, Vancouver ('83); Contributor to WCC multifaith study on Women, Religion and Sexuality ('90); Specialist in Biblical studies; Friend of slum dwellers; Warm and lively woman.

One evening I found myself in the back of a pick-up truck near Montevideo, Uruguay, hanging on for dear life as it hurtled over potholed roads toward one of the nearby slums. On arrival, Maria Teresa casually asked me to speak about Amos and what he had to say about the poor. Surrounding the truck were mothers of the "disappeared"; nuns working in the barrios; trade unionists from twenty-two poor neighborhoods; a progressive Catholic priest; and women from the nearby "base community"—a small community of the poor, brought together by their own human needs for shelter, food and water, and by Maria Teresa for Bible study! So I tried. I spoke to them about "justice roll[ing] on like a river and righteousness like an everflowing stream" (Amos 5.24 NEB). They spoke to me of how their poverty had more to do with an unfettered marketplace and the economic collapse of their country than with their so-called laziness. They spoke to me of the crushing foreign debt of their country, the repayment of which diverted money away from the needs of children.

What a remarkable woman she was! On a previous visit in 1986, she had taken me to visit another base community in the outskirts of Montevideo. It was a wasteland to my eyes. These people, displaced to make way for a super highway, lived in makeshift plastic shacks; mud was everywhere, and garbage and old plastic bags littered the landscape. I saw a ninety-year-old-woman lying on old car springs that were her bed. In front of her hovel was a desolate muddy field, host to rusted tin pails, discarded sanitary pads, stagnant pools, and stench. Many children had become "garbage pickers" for the family's survival. Half the babies died before age two. She had begun visiting these squatter's communities and gradually had them reading the Bible in the light of their own experience. She met great resistance at first, because the women had been treated to a litany of "what the Bible says." Be obedient. Be submissive. It's your fate to be poor. God will reward you in the next life.

Maria Teresa was a distinguished Catholic lay theologian who believed in practicing what she preached. She took a different approach from the 1980s conservative Latin American Catholics blessed by the Vatican, who accused the "base communities" of being communist in a time when that was a damning accusation. By the time I knew these women, they had discarded "the poor you shall have with you always" litany, as they studied the following text about Mary, Jesus' mother.

> *My soul magnifies the Lord, and my spirit rejoices in God my Saviour, for he has looked with favour on the lowliness of his servant. Surely, from now on all generations will call me blessed; For the Mighty One has done great things for me, and holy is his name. His mercy is for those that fear him from generation to generation. He has shown strength with his arm; he has scattered the proud in the thoughts of their hearts. He has brought down the powerful from their thrones, and lifted up the lowly; he has filled the hungry with good things, and sent the rich away empty.* (Luke 1.46–55 NRSV)

We Protestants tend to pay attention to Mary only at Christmas time when she appears in our pageants, draped in blue, tending her baby in the manger. How sweet! The women of the base community now identified with Mary as a young, vulnerable, destitute mother. They looked to her not only for comfort, but for a complete reversal of things as they were for them. They were no longer content with living off the discards of the rich: used spectacles, or second-hand clothing, or high heeled shoes. Their response to their poverty went far beyond begging for charity or even hope for self-reliance, to a raucous cry for just human relationships. When this base community took matters into its own hands, it did not deliver them from all poverty, but they now had hope and spiritual energy. Together they gathered local resources and managed to build two showers for the community; a day care centre for sixty-four children in a cramped shack; and a "popular pot—a large cauldron filled daily with vegetables and garbage leftovers and cooked over a wood fire. It was the only meal 150 children had, and they came at noon with their rusty tin-can plates, hoping no turnips had been included. The whole base community knew the changes could be sustained because they had done it! The women invited me to join them in a simple joyous dance, all the while singing "The Mother's Song," a musical rendition of the Magnificat taught to them by Maria Teresa.

Recently Protestant women have been learning a great deal about Mary from their Asian and Latin American Catholic colleagues. It is increasingly recognized that the redefinition of Mary is a task for all churches. Her song underlines the free choice of a fully liberated human being. Her "yes" to God places her in continuity with strong prophetic women who connect the history of Yahweh with the history of humanity's liberation. She stands alongside Puah and Shiprah, the Hebrew midwives who defied Pharaoh's cruel decree (Exodus 2) and won the deliverance of their people; with Miriam, who, along with Moses and Aaron, led the people into freedom, and who sings the oldest liberation song in the Bible (Exodus 15.20ff.). The names Mary and Miriam come from the same Hebrew root *marah*, which denotes obstinacy, contrariness, rebelliousness and revolt. It can also mean "plump" and "strong" which at that time was equivalent to "beauty." For 2000 years interpreters have presented the "beautiful" Mary. Contemporary women are opting for an interpretation that acknowledges the coexistence of "revolt" and "beauty."

When Mary sings her Magnificat she reveals her hope for radical transformation, for a new era, for a life lived in harmony with God's will. It bursts from the heartstrings of an oppressed people. So threatening is this to people in power that as recently as 1981 it was banned from the national radio network in Argentina by the military junta. When in 1980 the Polish workers scratched on the Lenin shipyard walls the slogan, "Madonna is on strike," they showed awareness of the Mary who rebelled. Challenges to the image of Mary as "up there," as crowned and standing on the moon, are being issued by women in Asia. "We reject Mary's hijacking by a wealthy church, for the consolation of the rich," they thunder. They look upon her as homeless, a refugee as they are, and a companion in their struggles.

Traditionally Mary's virginity has been understood by many biologically, which turns Jesus into a freak for contemporary women. We are not bound to think of the virgin birth as a physical event in order to believe that Jesus' whole life is of God. To read her virginity theologically is to affirm her as one of a kind, unique—the vehicle of the mystery of the Incarnation. Northrop Frye writes of someone who can "no longer 'believe in' the Virgin Birth" as one who "thinks he is saying that he can no longer honestly accept the historicity of the nativity stories in Matthew and Luke. But these stories do not belong to ordinary history at all: they form part of *Heilsgeschichte*, a mythical narrative…that cannot be assimilated to the historian's history. What he is really saying is that some elements in the gospel myth have less transforming power for him than others."[6] Frye goes on to say that disbelief in the Virgin Birth is not heresy but rather biblical illiteracy. Only fundamentalists read the gospels as though they are history, written down word for word as events took place.

So we return to Maria Teresa and her love of "the Mother's Song." She was appalled at the way people continue to respond to unjust economic situations largely through charity. Many mistake charity for justice. Maria Teresa worked with Canadian churches in the nineties, as we launched our "Year of Jubilee." Based on Leviticus 25, Jubilee refers to the fiftieth year, when all debts were cancelled, slaves set free, land rights of the poor honoured, and interest was not required from needy people (see the entry on Garth Legge on p. 36 of this book). The Canadian churches called for rich nations to fully forgive the debts of indebted nations. Presenting the proposal in the Senate at the time, I was told by another Senator that the program was unrealistic. Nevertheless it was later somewhat successful as in 2005 the richest countries did cancel the enormous debts the Most Indebted countries owed to the North. Maria Teresa would have said that the Madonna smiled with approval.

---

6   Northrop Frye, *The Double Vision: Language and Meaning in Religion* (Toronto: University of Toronto Press, 1991), p. 19.

Chapter 2
Resurrection

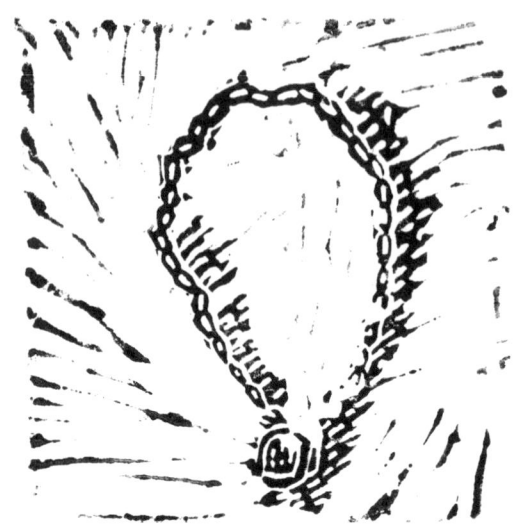

José Miguez Bonino, Argentina

5 March 1924 – 30 June 2012

Methodist pastor, theologian, ecumenist, human rights advocate, author; Ecumenical formation through World Student Christian Federation and Student Christian Movement; Doctorate in Theology from Union Theological Seminary, New York ('59); President, World Council of Churches ('75–83); Member Faith and Order Commission (WCC) for three decades; Director of ISEDET (Latin American Ecumenical Graduate Theological College); Delegate to Second Latin American Episcopal (Catholic) Conference, Medellin, Columbia ('68). Married to Noemi, three children.

"Thank you for your gift." "What gift?" I asked. "I have never met you before. I could not have given you a gift," I said. "Oh," they replied, "you met three of our group on Tuesday and gave them a silver pendant. Each of us wears the pendant for two weeks and then passes it to the next sister." I was meeting illegally with some of the Mothers of the "disappeared" young people, called the Mothers of May Square, in the basement of our partner Methodist church in Argentina. They were offering non-violent resistance to the military junta during the "dirty war" of 1976–83. I had just come from dictatorial South Korea, bearing a silver pendant from the brave women of the Presbyterian Church of the Republic of Korea, who had also been resisting dictators and military rule. The pendant was inscribed on one side with "Jesus Christ is Lord," and on the other, "Set the Prisoners Free."

May Square was the open space in front of the Presidential Palace. Every

Thursday, about one hundred mothers would walk arm in arm, silently, but crying out for news of their "disappeared" young people. Each wore a white headscarf bearing the name of her murdered child. On one occasion the military had been going to arrest two women, but when all the others insisted on being arrested too, the military backed down. Out of their individual pain they had forged themselves into a caring community. They transformed their private suffering into political consciousness and action. Their unique non-violent action lifted the brutality of the regime into the world spotlight.

Those committed to re-establishing democracy suffered betrayal, torture and "disappearance." Men were imprisoned for their political views, and retaliated with more resistance. Pro-democracy university students were abducted by the military and simply disappeared off the face of the earth. (Or in the ocean with their stomachs slit open.) Some were brutally tortured, their nails pulled out, their names and identities falsified, and the girls raped. Babies born to wrongfully imprisoned mothers were forcibly removed and "adopted" by the military to ensure indoctrination of a "proper" ideology. This was the price paid for working for democracy in Argentina at that time.

"The very essence of our faith is at stake," claimed José Miguez Bonino, a Methodist minister who played a central role in this resistance movement. Blacklisted by the military regime and risking crucifixion if arrested, he took the lead in restoring human rights.

I first met José Miguez Bonino on 21 Feb. 1978 at a lecture he gave in Toronto to those who supported the Ecumenical Forum, an agency committed to advancing progressive views of mission within Canadian churches. He had come at its invitation to challenge the theology and practice of Canadian churches in mission and ecumenism.

The only text at his funeral was,

> *Jews demand signs and Greeks desire wisdom, but we proclaim Christ crucified... to those who are the called...Christ the power of God and the wisdom of God.*
> (1Corinthians 1.22-24 NRSV)

How appropriate and perfectly aligned to his theological posture and thinking! He had always reaffirmed the centrality of Jesus Christ Crucified in our tradition. The message of appreciation at Miguez Bonino's funeral by Daniel Bruno said, "José talks about a Jesus Christ that doesn't tolerate preconceived moulds, but instead tries to break them to find what is new. This took him to the frontiers of thinking and pastoral practice."

This approach enabled him to defeat the decades of evangelical thinking in Latin America that identified evangelicals primarily by their opposition to Catholicism. It is difficult to convey the opposition, suspicion and even hatred that Catholics and Protestants had for each other at that time. In that poisonous atmosphere, through his understanding of Christ crucified, and all that meant in terms of vulnerability and non-violence to the "other," was a chance to recognize each other as sisters and brothers. Consequently, he was the only Protestant Latin American invited as an Observer to the Second Vatican Council.

This ecumenical thinking also enabled him to establish dialogue between Christians and Marxists in the 1960s as a response to the many Christians who were committed to fight for political freedom in Latin America. He helped many in Canada reframe their ecumenical search for unity and presented a new vision through his work and witness. It had to do with politicians, and constitutions as well. So Miguez Bonino worked to co-found The Permanent Assembly of Human Rights that denounced the atrocities of the crucifiers. He, a Christian minister and not a politician, was democratically elected as a member of the Constitutional Assembly. He worked on the reform of the 1994 Argentina Constitution to address the injustices of the previous decade, and to establish a democracy that guaranteed the rights of all citizens. He worked to eliminate the constitutional requirement that obliged all citizens who aspired to be president to be Catholic—not an insignificant accomplishment in a country where the Catholic hierarchy supported the military and consolidated power. He also ensured the recognition of the rights of aboriginal peoples in the renewed constitution. Here is his thinking about conversion.

"When a person is converted to Christ...he has not been invited to some sort of secluded soul fellowship," he wrote, "But he is converted to the One who defined His ministry as preaching good news to the poor, liberty to the captive, recovery of sight to the blind, setting the oppressed free, announcing the Lord's jubilee. This is the Christ of the gospel. And there is no other Christ to be converted to....What we need is a consistent and thorough-going conversion to the one God, to the one Christ of the Bible, not just adding to our distorted individualistic religion a dose, however generous, of social concern...and the cost...for the Canadian churches is a very heavy cost."[1]

---

1   José Miguez Bonino, *Mission as Conflict and Challenge*, The J. Lovell Murray Memorial Lecture, Innis College, University of Toronto (Toronto: Ecumenical Forum of Canada, 1978), n. pag.

He never identified what the cost would be, but like any good teacher, left that to us to figure out. I ponder whether we have abandoned all expectation of conversions to Christ in the sense that Miguez Bonino identifies, and settle instead for confirmation classes from which young people graduate out of the Christian community. Most troubling is the hesitation United Church people seem to have talking about Jesus at all. Is it because we think we will be perceived as fundamentalists? If we do find in Jesus Christ the meaning of the disconnected episodes of our lives, including their successes and failures, then why don't we talk about this?

Theologian Doug Hall wrote in the 2005 *United Church Observer*, "God's compassion for us is what the cross is all about; God's identification with us. For centuries the Christian church has been transfixed by a God who demanded sacrifice in atonement for our sins. Why this took over in Western Christendom is a great mystery. It didn't in the East."

So many hymns are still laced with what is called the "substitutionary theology of the atonement"—that Jesus took the rap for my sins so now I am free. He was the sacrificial lamb, the scapegoat depicted in gory detail in Mel Gibson's film" The Passion of Christ," which in my view is religious pornography. Jesus went to Jerusalem to demonstrate against the violent values of Imperial Rome, and the insidious collaboration of the high priests of the Temple with Rome, all of whom wanted to establish Pax Romana ("peace") through war. Jesus' way to peace through non-violence and love was in direct opposition to all of that, and resulted in his crucifixion. Does that not decisively reveal God's compassion for us, God's identification with the suffering in the world?

Hear Miguez Bonino's view of the meaning of the crucifixion for the church: "Poverty and economic justice; human rights and social justice, touch the very essence of the church...Such unity and such liberation we claim the Church can find today when she identifies with her Lord in committing herself to and participating with the poor in their own struggle for a new day for the whole of humankind...Theology cast in political terms has to concern itself with its relation to power."

How's that for understanding the crucifixion in a new way? How's that for those who claim religion and faith have nothing to do with political realities or power? How's that for you?

MARJORIE DAVIS (FREEMAN) CUMMINGS, CANADA

22 October 1924 – 24 March 1994

My older sister, twin to John; Nursing grad from Winnipeg General Hospital; Lived in small mining towns in Western Canada (Toby Creek, Ashcroft; Houston, Invermere, New Denver, all in BC); Committed Christian active in United Church of Canada; Community volunteer; Taught English to new immigrants; Expressed her faith through clowning; Active in Hospice; Supporter of UNICEF. Married to Webb, five children, nine grandchildren.

She was my older sister, yet not too much older to play with me with her cut-out paper dolls in the tent on rainy days. Her first summer job at the Gimli Fresh Air Camp in Manitoba opened the way for me to also work there the summer after Grade 12. She entertained me with her tales of delicious escapes from nursing authorities at the Winnipeg General Hospital when she defied the midnight curfews. She and a friend Helen Johnson biked from Winnipeg to Kenora, to my great envy. She always wanted to live in a city, but her husband's job predetermined small towns attached to mines in BC. I felt that I could say anything to her, or tell her anything, and she would not judge me. In short, she was my sister whom I loved.

> *Let the wilderness and the thirsty land be glad, let the desert rejoice and burst into flower. Let is flower with fields of asphodel, let it rejoice and shout for joy… Then shall blind men's eyes be opened, and the ears of the deaf unstopped. Then shall the lame man leap like a deer, and the tongue of the dumb shout aloud, for water springs up in the wilderness, and torrents flow in dry land. The mirage becomes a pool, the thirsty land bubbling springs; instead of reeds and rushes, grass shall grow in the rough land where wolves now lurk. And there shall be a causeway there which shall be called the Way of Holiness, and the unclean shall not pass along it; it shall become a pilgrim's way, no fool shall trespass on it. No lion shall come there; no savage beast climb on to it. Not one shall be found there. By it those he has ransomed shall return and the Lord's redeemed come home; they shall enter Zion with shouts of triumph, crowned with everlasting gladness. Gladness and joy shall be their escort, and suffering and weariness shall flee away.*
> (Isaiah 35.1–2a; 5–10 NEB)

What an entirely appropriate passage for my sister, who lived in semi-arid Ashcroft, which had rattlesnakes, wilderness, and thirsty ground. Yet she would also have seen it bloom sometimes. And how appropriate that this passage speaks also to those who battle despair and depression, as she did, and those who, as Marge put it, "live lives of quiet desperation." For the poet speaks of grace, compassion, and healing, which she also knew. She was deeply committed to sharing what she knew of healing with others with similar struggles. Troubled people looked to her for comfort and support. For floral tributes at her funeral she requested dandelions, because they were resilient, forcing their way through concrete, blooming everywhere regardless of efforts to stamp them out, cheerful splashes of colour. They were, after all, dandy lions. Marge expressed her faith through her clowning (her clowning name was "Bingo"), and the title page of her funeral bulletin had a photo of her in her clown costume, sporting a sign reading "Reduce, Reuse, Recycle."

And what a passage for the current faith community, somewhat immobilized by its search for survival of the church as institution. Canadian main line churches are experiencing a "drought," and the environment is under threat. Yet this passage promises restoration of the environment as well as its people. Promising hope and healing, it sounds the familiar Biblical theme of reversal, as Walter Brueggemann points out: "The blind will see! The deaf will hear! The lame will leap! The dumb will sing!"[2]

The imagery is of "a highway built across the wilderness land, so that God's beloved people...can return home in triumphant procession,"[3] a joyous homecoming along the causeway, the "Way of Holiness," as brokenness is healed, nature restored, and despair replaced by hope.

Marge chose another passage signaling hope:

> *I consider the sufferings of this present time are not worth comparing with the glory about to be revealed to us. For the creation waits with eager longing for the revealing of the children of God; for the creation was subjected to futility, not of its own will, but by the will of the one who subjected it, in the hope that the creation itself will be set free from its bondage to decay and will obtain the freedom of the glory of the children of God. We know that the whole creation has been groaning in labour pains until now; and not only creation but we ourselves, who have the first fruits of the Spirit grown inwardly while we wait for adoption, the redemption of our bodies. For in hope we are saved. Now hope that is seen is not hope. For who hopes for what is seen? But if we hope for what we do not see, we wait for it with patience.* (Romans 8.8–25 NRSV)

She hoped all her life—for things unseen and unrealized as do many of us. She would have felt so at home with the "dispossessed slum dwellers" of Buenos Aires, Argentina, with whom some Canadian theological students and myself visited in 1987. They had been displaced because of a super highway needed to transport tourists quickly from the airport to downtown. Now they lived in a "base community," served by a Catholic priest. They all contributed to their community, one being the collector of garbage, one the "sanitary engineer," one the keeper of the popular pot. They gathered regularly to read and search the scriptures for a Word that addressed their pitiful and hopeless situation. This passage from Romans was the one they asked us to share that night we visited them. Some in our group wanted them to pose for a photo, but they cried out, "No, come over and join us!" We are all in it together in this search and longing for hope. Just as Marge was in it together with all those who sought healing. Are you?

---

2   Walter Brueggemann, *Isaiah 1–39* (Louisville, KY: Westminster John Knox Press, 1998), p. 277.

3   Walter Brueggemann, *Isaiah 1–39*, p. 279.

Clifford A.S. Elliott, Canada

30 March 1919 – 27 February 2006

United Church minister; Author; Communicator; Saskatchewan roots in Langham; St. Andrews Theological College (Saskatoon); PhD in Literature of Religion from Union Theological Seminary, NY; Pastorates in Dundurn, Sask. ('42–'44); Third Ave N Battleford, Sask. ('47–'52); St Giles, Hamilton ('52–59); Robertson-Wesley, Edmonton ('59–'66); Metropolitan, Toronto ('66–'75); Bloor St., Toronto ('75–'86); Weekly radio commentator (CFRB-Toronto); Authored articles for *United Church Observer* ('60–'90); Weekly column for *Toronto Star*; Mounted Festival of the Arts and left family legacy of music; Travelled all continents extensively; After retirement, a volunteer chaplain at Casey House (HIV/AIDS hospice) and Wellesley Hospital (HIV/AIDS wing); Holidayed in Haliburton; Married to Patricia ('42, deceased in '77), four children, five grandchildren. Married to Mary ('84); Suffered stroke during routine surgery and profound memory loss ('95).

Cliff had a heart attack in December, 1995. He wrote, "In the hospital I had to ask, 'Why was my life saved? Why, for that matter was it given in the first place?' Now, I had to ask, 'What new rhythm shall I set for this renewing heart? Of what good is a new heart to an old life?'...after the resurrection of Jesus, some disciples said merely, 'Let's go back fishing.' But the Book of Acts tells another story. The disciples...proclaimed the Resurrection as a fact of life....My question now is not simply, 'How soon can I resume my former way of life, go back fishing?' It is instead: 'How can this battered, scarred, but miraculously renewed heart beat the beat of the heart of God?'"[4]

For me, that pretty much sums up Cliff Elliott. His belief in resurrection was not just a belief in a future life, a life after death. It was belief in a quality of life and relationships that lasts forever, that transcends whatever happens during our brief lives, because it is firmly rooted in eternity. He knew how to live in the midst of death. He was a gifted, passionate preacher, anchoring his sermons in life experiences. He experienced profound loss through the death of his first wife, two brothers and two sisters, and a daughter. He rejected the kind of theology that declared God sent him his daughter Gracie, who had Down Syndrome, to teach him a special kind of love. He believed that God's love is available to all without restrictions, and that God does not single out particular individuals such as the differently abled to teach us the availability and necessity of generous love.

Once a week he visited with relatives of people who had HIV/AIDS. He volunteered as a chaplain at Casey House, which housed victims of HIV/AIDS in Toronto. He believed that if Christians had not chosen the cross as their central symbol, they might well have chosen the towel, remembering Jesus' act of washing the feet of his disciples recorded in John's gospel. He was a first class preacher, who wandered the aisles of the church while speaking the good news directly to congregants.

He was a feminist. In 1979 he supported the hanging in the chancel of Bloor Street United Church the sculpture Crucified Woman[5] on Good Friday. Despite accusations of heresy and scandal, angry phone calls from as far away as the southern U.S.A. and people yelling against it outside the church, he remained adamant that it remain on Easter Day. "This has been the most excruciating Holy Week in all of my ministry. But never has this congregation talked so much about Christ and about suffering....I feel as if I'm just beginning to see the world through the eyes of women."[6] In 1986 amidst more controversy, the sculpture found its final place in the courtyard of Emmanuel College, Toronto.

After the stroke he suffered during routine surgery, his wife Mary decided

---

4 Clifford A. S. Elliott, *Apples of Gold* (Toronto: Clifford A. S. Elliott, 2000), p. 96.
5 See the entry on Margaret Laurence on p. 69 of this book.
6 Doris Jean Dyke, *Crucified Woman* (Toronto: The United Church Publishing House, 1991), p. 5.

to keep him at home. She built a special room on to their house, and there he remained until his death. Whenever I visited him, he would respond at great length and some depth to a theological inquiry, since that had been his major lifelong preoccupation, but not to current affairs, since that part of his brain addressing contemporary issues appeared to have been irretrievably damaged by his stroke. I often wonder what he would have written for the *Toronto Star* about his debilitating life should he have been able.

Of a number of texts chosen for his funeral, I have decided to comment on Isaiah 6.1-8. Cliff used this text to preach many a Church anniversary service, as believers were commissioned to put themselves at God's disposal for mission.

> *In the year of King Uzziah's death I saw the Lord high and seated on a throne, high and exalted, and the skirt of his robe filled the temple. About him were attendant seraphim, and each had six wings; one pair covered his face and one pair covered his feet, and one pair was spread in flight. They were calling ceaselessly to one another, "Holy, holy, holy is the Lord of Hosts: the whole earth is full of his glory." And, as each one called, the threshold shook to its foundations, while the house was filled with smoke. Then I cried, "Woe is me! I am lost, for I am a man of unclean lips and I dwell among a people of unclean lips; yet with these eyes I have seen the King, the Lord of Hosts." Then one of the seraphim flew to me carrying in his hands a glowing coal which he had taken from the altar with a pair of tongs. He touched my mouth with it and said, "See this has touched your lips; your iniquity is removed, and your sin is wiped away." Then I heard the Lord saying, "Whom shall I send? Who will go for me?" And I answered, Here am I; send me.*
>
> (Isaiah 6.1-8 NEB)

The text raises two questions for us. What is meant by mission? "And I said, 'Here I am; send me.'" "Sending" has usually been associated with what we call "mission," which has for a long time meant northern and western churches sending personnel to the global south churches. Now, mature Christians from Ghana, Columbia and other developing countries have arrived on our shores, wishing to associate with us in mutual reciprocal ministry. Will we welcome them as equals and graciously accept their gifts to us?

The other question is what does it mean to put oneself at God's disposal? For Cliff, it clearly meant venturing into lots of unknown territory to him. For him, it was sitting with those with HIV/AIDS, talking with prostitutes, visiting prisoners, listening to the story of the unemployed, being with unlikely people in improbable places.

And for us? I have heard many a sermon on how wonderful it was for Simon Peter, Andrew, James and John to immediately leave their fishing nets to follow Jesus when he called them to fish for people. No one ever asks how their wives felt when they discovered their husbands had taken this precipitous action. No one ever asks why they could not "fish for people" by remaining in their given situation as fishermen. They must have met many people in the course of their day—in the market, on the beaches, in the villages. Why was it so praiseworthy to leave their ordinary jobs to follow Jesus? Do not some folk enter ordained ministry thinking that it is a more worthy vocation than sticking with their job at IBM, or at the local high school? Is not Christian calling primarily (although not always) a calling to faithfulness in our own situation, not one we think is more worthy than ours? What has happened to our recognition of the ministry of the laity? Do we no longer honour the priesthood of all believers?

Cliff said, "A lot of us seem to think we are destined to live nothing but thoroughly ordinary lives—to be nothing but ordinary people. But, as the Hebrews proved, even ordinary people—everybody, in fact—can set a goal, can choose standards, and can accept God's gracious promise to travel with them. Perhaps we resist that truth because it lacks the colour and the fame that more spectacular events and achievements seem to offer. It is humbling to learn that it is in being faithful in our ordinary lives that we prove what is so unique about us."[7]

A woman once told me of a time when she was very ill: "My friend visited me in the hospital. I wondered why she came, seeing as I could not hear or feel. But suddenly it dawned on me that her coming had been an act of friendship, when sometimes without knowing it, we ordinary people praise God."

---

7   Clifford A. S. Elliott, *Apples of Gold*, p. 128.

E. G. D. (Gard) Freeman, Canadian
11 March 1890 – 20 March 1973

My father; Professor of Systematic and Practical Theology and Professor of Christian Ethics ('38–'46) and Dean of Theology, United College, Winnipeg ('46–'58); Degrees from Knox College, Toronto ('15) and Post-grad Fellowship at Columbia University, NY; three pastorates at St. Enoch's, Toronto ('16–'21); King Memorial, Winnipeg ('20–'30) and St. Paul's, Thunder Bay ('30–'38); Independent thinker; Hospitable open house in Winnipeg; Uniquely combined theory and practice of theology. Married to my mother, Ada; five children, of whom I was the youngest, 21 grandchildren.

"Where in the hell are we?" shouted a man from the large boat loaded with people and obviously lost on Lake of the Woods. The boat was big enough to risk shipwreck if it approached our small island any closer. "You're not in hell at all," my father shouted back. "You're just in purgatory." That was my Dad, known popularly as "Gard." He was to become my Professor in Theology at United College (now the University of Winnipeg), where I studied to become a minister.

At age eleven he had presented himself before the Session of Erskine Presbyterian Church in Toronto to "join the church." How could he know what he was doing? It took personal interviews with four different elders and several long sessions with the minister to convince them of his readiness. He was received into full communion, as was the custom, with a handshake—the extension of the "right hand of Christian fellowship."

One of the greatest gifts given to me by my Dad was the annual canoeing and tenting holiday, beginning for me at the age of three months. These featured our parents and five children (frequently augmented with a few friends) paddling a twenty-foot freighter canoe from one undeveloped campsite to another on Lake of the Woods, or Lake Nipigon, or Lake Superior, or Lac des Mille Lacs. We never saw mainland for a month, taking all necessary supplies with us and augmenting the diet with fish and berries. Etched in my memory is the night we sailed up Lake of the Woods from Whitefish Bay to Kenora by moonlight, to a steady comforting breeze. I had helped my Dad hoist the same blanket that covered us at night as a sail, and although I was just a kid, he let me control the sheet and the steering. I came to love the water, the rocks, the wind, the trees, the flowers, the animals and the stars, and to look upon the silences, the solitude, and the spaciousness as essential to my maturing spirituality. For me, as to him, it was an annual refreshment of soul and body.

My parents had met in 1908 at Harbord Collegiate Institute in Toronto, and a prized possession of my family is a scribbled note to Ada from Gard, "meet me at noon. If not, what about four?" Mother was less keen and persuaded her friend to walk home between her and her ardent suitor. Eight years later they were married. Their relationship in later life is so well expressed in George Eliot's *Adam Bede*, "What greater thing is there for two human souls than to feel that they are joined for life—to strengthen each other in all labour, to rest on each other in all sorrow, to minister to each other in all pain, to be one with each other in silent unspeakable memories at the moment of the last parting?"[8]

A man of many parts, he could fix a broken-down car, or the ripped canvas of a canoe with spruce gum, develop photographs in the bathtub, identify every tree in the forest and every star in the heavens, or discuss Hegel or theologian Karl Barth.

As Professor of Practical Theology at United College in later years, he approved the central pulpit, situated above the table that reinforced architecturally his conviction that preaching the Word informed the sacraments. He had a healthy disdain of conformity and printed prayers or ceremonies, but a sound conviction that serious and careful preparation were therefore most necessary. Believing preaching was essentially an oral skill, he told our class on

---

8   George Eliot, *Adam Bede* (New York: New American Library, 1961), p. 501.

Preaching: "If you can't remember what you will be saying for the next fifteen minutes, how do you expect the congregation to remember anything?" He would regale us with stories of pastorates that were "all front and no back." His commitment to a life of self-giving showed itself in the perpetual stream of students, unemployed, sick or damaged people, and missionaries on leave from Norway House in northern Manitoba that became our extended family. His home, at 710 Dorchester, Winnipeg, was known as Grand Central Station. Unnumbered people across Canada had access to our eleven-room house in Winnipeg, as each had a duplicate front door key. During my formative years, United Church personnel back from Africa, India, or China were frequent guests in my parents' home. They opened up vistas I had never imagined and from them I gained my first impression that I was not the centre of the universe after all.

He spoke of ministry as a calling and vocation, not a job. He believed in spreading the good news, so every Sunday afternoon he would head out of town to small villages where he started new congregations. I went along, and loved what was obviously for him exhilarating, fulfilling, and fun. So it is no wonder that years later, I chased people from my Moderator's office when they came to inform me that a day consisted of three blocks of time, and I was to be at work only in two of those blocks. My father also believed "God so loved the world," so he spent a lot of time with many who were not pillars of the church, such as trade unionists, capitalist business men, or the un-churched, like Tim Buck, leader of the Communist Party.

His death was an affirmation of life. I should not have been surprised at the way he died, because it was perfectly consistent with the way he had lived. It made no sense to him to prolong life just for the sake of prolonging it. He asked us, his children, to help him die. He asked us to make sure the hospital staff didn't bring him any more unwanted trays of food. It was almost as though he were impatient to be on the other side of life. He continued to express his love and care for those he would leave behind. Even on his deathbed, he made his five children laugh, and we returned the favour. He fell into a coma. The hands that had offered the cup of salvation and the bread of life to so many fell useless at his side. I had an extraordinary sense of the mystery of both birth and death being cut from the same cloth—the warning pains, the intensity of them growing stronger, the negotiation of the final passage, and then the emergence of a new reality and affirmation of the continuity of life. I remembered one of his favourite Biblical texts, "So we never lose heart," which was later used at his funeral.

> *For we do not proclaim ourselves; we proclaim Jesus Christ as Lord and ourselves as your slaves for Jesus' sake…But we have this treasure in clay jars, so that it may be made clear that this extraordinary power belongs to God and does not come from us. We are afflicted in every way, but not crushed; perplexed, but not driven to despair; persecuted, but not forsaken; struck down, but not destroyed; always carrying in the body the death of Jesus, so that the life of Jesus may also be made visible in our bodies…So we do not lose heart. Even though our outer nature is wasting away, our inner nature is being renewed day by day. For this slight momentary affliction is preparing us for an eternal weight of glory beyond all measure, because we look not at what can be seen but at what cannot be seen; for what can be seen is temporary, but what cannot be seen is eternal.* (2 Corinthians 4:5, 7–10, 16–18 NRSV)

He knew crushing disappointment in his life when one of his leading congregants turned out to have clay feet. He knew it again when the United Church stripped the theological college in Winnipeg of its MD degree-giving status he had worked so hard to establish over twenty years, as the church consolidated its theological colleges across the country. One of his sons was alienated from him for much of his lifetime. He was perplexed by those who rejected the gospel or the church out-of-hand, but he never fell into despair. He knew ministry was not about him. He knew the treasure was in clay jars. He had always known it.

Dad believed that the invisible things like love, mercy and compassion had more reality than those things we can readily see. Theologian Walter Brueggemann writes eloquently along the same lines. He writes of the two worlds in which we live simultaneously: the presumed world of everyday chores, happenings, sadness, and bad news, and the proposed world of compassion, mercy, love, and good news that Jesus announces. We are invited to live in this everyday world in such a way that is it informed by the proposed world into which Jesus invites us. Is the proposed world of compassion and mercy and love the only authentic reality, though invisible? Is this what Paul means by the phrase, "what we cannot see is eternal?" When compassion or love or mercy sometimes becomes visible in our presumed world through faithful people, it astonishes and amazes us. It is then we know its "eternal" lasting reality. My Dad knew that. "So we do not lose heart." Not a bad text for contemporary Christians living in a world much in need of the unseen realities of justice and love becoming a reality.

Margaret Laurence, CC, Canada

18 July 1926 – 5 January 1987

Renowned Canadian feminist novelist and essayist; Educated United College, Winnipeg ('47); Lived in England ('49), Somaliland ('50–'52), Gold Coast, later Ghana, ('52–'57), Vancouver '57–'62, England for 10 more years; then Lakefield, Ontario; Author of 16 books including *The Stone Angel* ('64); Winner of Governor General's Awards for *A Jest of God* ('66) and *The Diviners* ('74); Chancellor Trent Univeristy ('81–'83); buried in Neepawa, MB ('87). Married and divorced, two children.

Who on earth was that woman who, in English class, monopolized the floor by posing unanswerable questions to the English professor? It was 1944, and a smattering of seventeen-year-old straight-out-of-high-school types, including myself and the questioner, found ourselves in the same small English class with a number of service personnel returning to civilian life after World War II. Why did she pose such difficult questions? And why did the professor turn all his attention to the question? It was when she started to publish some of her poems in VOX, the undergraduate College publication, that I discovered her name was Peggy Wemyss, later known as Margaret Laurence.

The scene was United College (now the University of Winnipeg.) While I was involved in sports and the Student Christian Movement, Margaret wrote poetry and short stories, avoided religious institutions, wrote for VOX, and worked part time at *The Citizen*, a left wing daily newspaper. Our paths crossed frequently, however, through numerous conversations and debates in "Tony's," the College cafeteria, about student politics, about opposition to unjust social causes, and about the best ways to save the world. Our value systems were hammered out in those days over coffee and long discussions.

After graduation we saw each other infrequently. There were many years when we were not in touch at all. Yet when we did meet, we continued the conversations that had engaged us previously. In the winter of 1977, Roy received a call at his Hamilton church office. "This is someone out of your Winnipeg past. You may not remember me but I remember you and Lois and would like to come for a visit since I am at a book-signing downtown. My name is Margaret Laurence."

As if we didn't know she was now a famous Canadian novelist and one of the first Canadian feminist authors who wrote books and crafted characters through the eyes of women. Her book *The Stone Angel*, about the life of an elderly woman of the prairies, Hagar, had become a Canadian classic. And as if we didn't know she had just been awarded the Governor General's Award for *The Diviners* in 1974. We were delighted she was coming, and both my university-aged daughters hastily cancelled their plans for that evening and came racing home to be part of that visit.

A few days after her visit she wrote, "It was so very good to see you and Roy and talk with you. Amazing how the years fell away and yet in some ways it was because of the very varied experiences of myself and you two during those years that seemed at this point to have brought us quite close in outlook and perceptions. I felt as you did—incredibly 'warmed' by the evening."

She was one of the first feminist authors writing from the perspective of female characters, and she was attacked for her depiction of the seamy side of life, including the liberal use of profanity by her characters. During the decade of the 70s, she was eternally thankful for the support she received from the Anglican and United church members in Lakefield, Ontario, where she lived when her books were attacked as pornographic. She sorrowed greatly because her critics did not grasp the profound morality and the passionate ethical themes of justice, peace, and racial discrimination that her novels explored. In the end, the attacks prompted her to re-examine her relationship with Lakefield United Church, which she cautiously re-entered.

She told me what had brought her back to the church. "It was the God language that spoke of the Holy Spirit as feminine," she said. "That hymn 'Father-like He tends and spares us'[9] sounds like a mother to me, even if it is using male imagery." "I have a feeling," she said in a conversation with me (excerpted in the Feb. 1980 *United Church Observer*, p. 11), that "there has to be more recognition of the kind of female principle in God. I don't mean people going around with T-shirts saying, 'Trust in the Lord, She will provide.' That is a trivial way of looking at it. But after centuries of thinking of God in strictly male, rather authoritarian terms, it seems to me there has to be some recognition of the female principle in God." This is not an earth-shaking statement today. But at the time, it represented a significant break with traditional theology by a distinguished author.

Because she knew the sculptress, Margaret was supportive of having the statue of the Crucified Woman[10] displayed in Bloor Street United Church. Every 6 Dec. on the anniversary of the 1989 Montreal massacre of fourteen female engineering students shot in cold blood by Marc Lepine, people have gathered around that statue remembering the vulnerability of God and the continuing crucifixion of women.

A phone call on Thanksgiving weekend in 1986 alerted me to her impending death. My son Bruce took the call, and left me a scribbled note saying that Margaret had phoned and she didn't sound so great. She had been diagnosed with terminal cancer, suffered from alcoholism, and knew her time was limited. She had phoned to ask if I would bury her when the time came. Her subsequent death, while self-inflicted, was for her an affirmation of life, a positive decision.

In our final visit, Margaret was at once grieving, raging, dancing, jubilating, and rejoicing, as we planned her funeral service. For hymns she settled on "Guide Me, O Thou Great Jehovah" (VU #651). "I want that one partly because it expresses some of my life's struggle for peace and justice, and partly because it reminds me of the old Welsh coalminers singing it as they marched up Whitehall in 1929, seeking better working conditions," she said. The service was to conclude with "All People That on Earth Do Dwell" (VU #822), using the Version in the Scottish Psalter of 1650. She wished to have scriptural texts from both Testaments. She

---

9   "Praise, My Soul, the King of Heaven," *The Hymnary of the United Church of Canada* (Toronto: The United Church Publishing House, 1930), #17. VU#240 provides a revised version of the hymn, "Praise, My Soul, the God of Heaven."
10 See the entry on Clifford A.S. Elliott on page 61 of this book.

then showed me her scribbled commentary in the margins of her 1795 family Bible, evidence of the vigorous conversations she carried on with God. Years later, I recognized that I had learned such a practice from her, and that my jottings would become the seeds of this book. The following text reflects her lifelong posture of thanksgiving.

> *Rejoice always, pray without ceasing, give thanks in all circumstances; for this is the will of God in Christ Jesus for you. Do not quench the Spirit.*
> (1 Thessalonians 5.16–19 NRSV)

In her book *The Stone Angel*, Margaret writes of the last days of Hagar, an elderly woman. Hagar's daughter-in-law Doris has arranged for a clergyman, Mr. Troy, to visit Hagar in the hospital. After it becomes obvious that Mr. Troy knows only how to drone in a monotonous voice when he prays, Hagar interrupts to ask if he knows the hymn that starts out "All people that on earth do dwell," and will he sing it to her now, by her bedside? Stunned as he is by the request, he accedes, and sings with a beautiful voice,

> *All people that on earth do dwell,*
> *Sing to the Lord with cheerful voice.*
> *Him serve with mirth, His praise forth tell;*
> *Come ye before Him and rejoice.*

Hagar responds, "I would have wished it....I must always, always have wanted that—simply to rejoice. How is it I never could?"[11]

Margaret reflected the healthy tension that a person of faith lives between the present unsatisfactory state of the world and the longed-for transformation that is promised. She would have loved the text that enjoins us to "rejoice always." The text goes on to say, "give thanks in all circumstances." Even with a terminal cancer diagnosis, a deteriorating health, and an enormous thigh-high plaster cast immobilizing her? My last conversation with her was, "Life is for rejoicing—for dancing." With tears streaming down her face, out of a mixture of physical weakness and intense emotion, she cried out to me, "And I've danced.

---

11 Margaret Laurence, *The Stone Angel* (Toronto: McClelland and Stewart: 1964), pp. 291–92.

I've danced." For her that was the meaning of our short and vulnerable lives. What a different emphasis this is from faith communities that emphasize sin, sorrow, and gloom.

But the text asks us to rejoice in all circumstances, good and bad. We are not invited to give thanks for circumstances, but in circumstances. This raises important unanswerable questions for many. How could rejoicing be possible for Elie Wiesel in a Nazi concentration camp? How possible for a mother in Syria who watches her children being bayoneted without mercy? Or the aboriginal "missing" women in Canada who were unmercifully abused before "disappearing?" How can we or they rejoice in the face of such gross injustice, suffering and despair?" Perhaps the question can only be answered by people in those situations. Let's be clear that we do not rejoice for all of the savagery. But we need to ponder how to give thanks in its midst.

The passage ends with "quench not the Spirit," that same Spirit that provokes us to resist injustice and us to establish justice on earth. Look for what the Spirit is already doing. Join your life to the work of the Spirit. Live faithfully. Don't give up just because it looks pretty bleak. Rejoice always in God's intention of peace for all peoples and for this world, even in the midst of terror and death. Work to establish justice and peace, recognizing that the Spirit is already at work in the world. Surely a cause for rejoicing.

Alexander Udny Lind, Canada
1915 – 2007

A Homily in Celebration of the Life of Alexander Udny Lind, by his son Christopher Lind, 16 January 2007. (Used by permission)

And all the people responded with a great shout when they praised the Lord, because the foundation of the house of the Lord was laid. But many of the priests and Levites and heads of families, old people who had seen the first house on its foundations, wept with a loud voice when they saw this house, though many shouted aloud for joy, so that the people could not distinguish the sound of the joyful shout from the sound of people's weeping, for the people shouted so loudly that the sound was heard far away. (Ezra 3.11–13 NRSV)

I pray that the words I speak and the words you hear will do honour to God: Father, Son and Holy Spirit. Amen.

The first reading today is taken from the book of Ezra. It tells the story of Jerusalem after a long period of civil war. Eventually Israel was invaded by the Chaldeans and they destroyed the centre of religious life (the first Temple in Jerusalem). The Israelites were then sent into a long period of exile in Babylon. Eventually the Temple was rebuilt under the orders of the King Cyrus of Persia and the Israelites began to return. This passage tells the story of the pain and destruction of war, the longing to rebuild society and then the mixed emotions of the elderly when the new society emerges to replace the old.

There are many people here today who were born or grew up in wartime. Your stories will echo the stories of my father who was born in the war time of 1915. He was orphaned before he finished high school and went overseas to begin his life anew. At the age of 24 he was thrust back into the 2nd World War with experiences the depth of which he never shared but sometimes hinted at with his children. The next 60 years of his life were spent re-building and remembering, as he was able. Today we still live in a time of war, children are still being orphaned and God continues to call us to choose life over death, and to re build community, to rebuild the Temple out of the ashes of death, destruction and loss.

Alec rebuilt family life with our mother Anne Williams, and five children. He rebuilt the insurance business with the New Zealand Insurance Company in Hong Kong, Singapore, and then Canada. In the mid-fifties he helped lay the cornerstone of an expanded St. Jude's Anglican Church as a warden, with Canon Fred Jackson. We especially appreciate the effort of the current and former wardens of St. Jude's to honour that leadership role with their participation in the service today. He was in his early forties when that happened and I sometimes wonder at the energy he found for that task with the challenges of an expanding business and children at home aged 1, 3, 4, 7, and 9.

Twenty years later he was joining the ranks of the ancients. He had lived past the age his mother died and past the age his father died. He retired at 62. Now there was a new generation of leaders trying to rebuild the church. They re-translated the Bible, created alternatives to the Prayer Book, sold off the cemetery, sold off the rectory and put the military flags behind glass. He witnessed all these changes and opposed them. In biblical terms, he wept. I consider Ian Dingwall to have been a great rector of this parish but he initiated many of the changes my father opposed. I remember Ian telling me once that he fought hard to have the military flags removed from the nave entirely and put in the hall. All he managed, he said, was to have them put under glass. Following this decision, my father was absent from worship for several weeks. When he finally re-appeared, Ian expressed relief to him because he feared he had driven Alec away. My father had simply been travelling, but when he heard this, he looked Ian up and down and said, "Ian, rectors come and go, but this is my church, and you'll have to work a lot harder than that to get me to leave. The new church was being built just like the

Second Temple and many people were rejoicing, but some people, especially the old people like my father, who had seen the first house on its foundations were weeping. This weeping did not prevent him from coming to St Jude's every week once, twice, and finally, in his wandering illness, five times a day. In the middle of conflict and weeping, St. Jude's was his home and as a family we rejoice with thanksgiving at the warm reception he always received here.

There are many references in Scripture to the body being like a Temple for the Holy Spirit (1 Cor. 6.19). We are exhorted to honour the body like a temple and in John's gospel (John 2.21) Jesus' body is likened to a Temple that when destroyed will be raised up in three days. You may be interested to know that my father believed in the physical resurrection of the body. Like so many others, this is what he was taught so many years ago and so this is what he believed. Unfortunately he was never taught what I was taught and what I teach, which is to ask which body he expected to be resurrected? Would it be the 17 year-old who won the Hammersmith rowing championship on the Thames River in England? Or would it be the 25 year-old sworn to secrecy as he prepared for the Japanese invasion of Malaya? Somehow I don't think he imagined it would be the diseased and bed-ridden body we have cradled in recent days.

As we get older it becomes apparent to all of us that our identity is fixed with a certain age. For some of us we are always 18; for others always 32. We look in the mirror and wonder who is this grey-haired person staring back at me. My father once told me that inside he was always 29. That was 1944, the year he married my mother.

I believe in the Resurrection and I believe in life after death. I like to think that the body that will rise today has the gentleness of a man in his eighties, the courage of a man in his twenties, and the good looks of a man in his thirties and forties. I know he is bound to have the same sense of loyalty, duty, and faithfulness he exhibited all his life. We are here today to testify that a new temple is indeed being built, but amid the shouts of joy you will also hear the voices of some who weep as they remember the first house on its foundation. Amen.

Bertha Margaret McMahon, Canada

5 June 1910 – 29 July 2003

Clothing designer for bridal gowns at the Hudson's Bay Company in Winnipeg; Member of United Church of Canada by choice; Clerk of Session for Atlantic Avenue United Church, Winnipeg; Wife and Mother of one; Forthright and generous person.

I knew Bertha ("Bert") McMahon in Winnipeg, at Atlantic Avenue United Church where Roy and I ministered (1953-59). I once remarked to someone, "Bert visits the sick and the widows, and pays attention to people on the fringes." She was one of the first people I encountered who actually did this. She had a remarkably deep spirituality, a great sense of humour, and left no one in doubt as to what she thought. As one of the rare female Clerks of Session at the time, she offered support and wise counsel to a young minister and his wife (as I was then known!) just starting on a lifetime in ordained ministry.

She was employed by "The Bay" department store prior to her marriage. Most of us sewed Singer sewing machine clothes for our families, but wedding gowns were another matter. She designed and sewed wedding gowns by hand for the Hudson's Bay choice customers. They came "out of her head" and her fertile imagination, and not from some cookie cutter pattern developed by someone else. Her daughter Catherine told me that she always wanted to go to New York and be a fashion designer, but she was born too soon. In her day, convention decreed that married women didn't work, so she had to leave the Hudson's Bay Company's employment when she married. However, all her life she designed and sewed exquisite clothes for her family and some others.

One of the passages of scripture read at her funeral was the following,

> *Let not your hearts be troubled; ye believe in God, believe also in me. In my Father's house are many mansions.* (John 14.1–2 KJV)

> *If it were not so, would I have told you that I go to prepare a place for you? And if I go and prepare a place for you, I will come again and will take you to myself, so that where I am, there you may be also. And you know the way to the place where I am going. Thomas said to him, "Lord, we do not know where you are going. How can we know the way?" Jesus said to him, "I am the way, and the truth, and the life. No one comes to the Father except through me. If you know me, you will know my Father also. From now on you do know him and have seen him."* (John 14.2–8 NRSV)

Bertha was adamant. "In my Father's House are many mansions," it reads—so please use the translation that says "mansions." It's not going to be a rooming house!" She was quite sure of this, as she was convinced that the welcome would be sumptuous and generous. Committed to the finest workmanship and the best bridal gowns possible, she concluded that faithful arrivals in "my Father's House" could expect the same attention to fine detail and magnificent surroundings. Continuity was assured, and care and hospitality guaranteed.

The latter part of the passage presents difficulties to some, which Bertha could not have anticipated. In her day, Buddhists and Muslims were people about whom we infrequently heard. It seems to say that Jesus is the exclusive way to salvation. "I am the way, and the truth and the life. No one comes to the Father except through me." What could be clearer, particularly if you are used to using proof texts to bolster your opinion? But it contradicts all we know of Jesus from other gospels—his ability to break barriers, to include everyone. So how are we to understand this text? We are not fundamentalists, so need to look at the context, which is a tiny, non-confident community struggling for its identity in the Jewish community in an Hellenic world.

Diana Eck, director of the Pluralism Project at Harvard, poses the question,

"If 'I am the Way' is the answer, what exactly was the question?"[12] Thomas, along with the other disciples, was worried and anxious about the future. Jesus was about to disappear from their midst. How would he know what to do? He was surely not asking about the fate of the Muslims, or the Jews, or the Hindus. "On that night of uncomprehending uncertainty he asked, 'Lord, we do not know where you are going; how can we know the way?' And Christ answered, 'I *am* the Way,...' It was a pastoral answer, not a polemical one. It was an expression of comfort, not condemnation."[13]

So often Christians have used it as a club to clobber those of other faiths or agnostics and atheists. Jesus as "the Way" is the way of love, and to that Way we are called, as were those disciples. But it goes on, "No one comes to the Father but by me." How can this be lived out in a multi-religious context such as we have in Canada? For Christians, the way to God is through Jesus Christ and his way of love. No other way will do for us. That is an expression of what we have seen and known in our own lives. That is our faith commitment. Just as I believe my birth father to be "the best father in all the world," in my view, it doesn't exclude your father. The language of love is being used in this text, and we do well to recognize that. But that doesn't mean we demonize and exclude all others. There are many mansions. It doesn't mean no other faith family is known to God. The Hindus, with 5,000 years of history, have rich experiences of holiness to share. Theirs is also a valid and full tradition. Knowing how to love is not the exclusive practice of Christians.

Here is a poem reprinted by permission of Stanley Samartha, at one time staff person of the WCC "Dialogue with Other Faiths" Department. He wrote me that this poem has touched many more people across the world than his theological articles.

Why Did I Look Back? [14]

*I was afraid of the two strangers
who came to our house last evening.
They said "we" were good.*

---

12 Diana L. Eck, *Encountering God: A Spiritual Journey from Bozeman to Banaras* (Boston: Beacon Press, 1993), p. 94.
13 Diana L. Eck, *Encountering God*, p. 94.
14 See Lois M. Wilson, *Stories Seldom Told: Biblical Stories Retold for Children and Adults* (Kelowna, BC: Northstone, 1977), pp. 166-67.

But "they," our neighbours, were bad.
Lot was so pleased
That he did a big "namaste"[15] *to them*
And asked me to prepare a feast.
Lot said they were angels, but I was afraid of them.
Their faces were cold, their looks harsh, and their eyes were
burning with anger.

Why did I look back?

I was angry at Lot.
When the men surrounded our house
and wanted the strangers to come out,
Lot offered to send our virgin daughters to them.
But both girls were engaged to be married.
I was angry. Very angry. Outraged.
I pushed them into the little storeroom at the back.
I stood guard over against it. Over my dead body.
When those men wanted men, why send girls to them?
Why didn't Lot himself go?
Why didn't the two angels go?
That would have been an angelic happening.

Why did I look back?

Because my neighbours were out there.
When, during the birth of my first child, I cried out in pain,
the women were there.
They held my hands, wiped my brow.
Gave me water to drink. And when the baby was born,
they bathed it and put it to my breast.

---

15 Hindu greeting or welcome.

And where was Lot?
He was out in the fields praying to his God.

When my little girl hit her foot against a stone
And broke her toenail,
my neighbours came with some crushed leaves,
And put them in her tea. My daughter smiled through tears.

And where was Lot?
He was out in the fields praying to his God.

You say only the women were good, but the men were bad?
When there was no water for three days
And my children were crying,
My neighbour's husband walked three miles to get water
And then he gave us some.

Why did I look back?

Because I wanted to perish with my neighbours,
Rather than be saved without them.

Bertha McMahon was confident that "in my Father's house" there are many mansions. Are you?

Dorothee Sölle, Germany

30 September 1929 – 27 April 2003

German liberation theologian; Feminist; Author; Poet; Radical Christian; Coined term "Christofascism" to identify fundamentalist Christians; Doctorate in the connections between poetry and theology; University lecturer in Cologne and Mainz; Actively opposed Vietnam war, the arms race of the Cold War, and injustices in the developing world; Organized "Political Night Prayers" in Cologne ('68–'72); Prof of Systematic Theology at Union Theological Seminary, NY. ('75–'87). Married to Fulbert Steffensky, four children.

We feminists had to be as wise as serpents and as innocent as doves to have Dorothee Sölle finally accepted as a speaker at the World Council of Churches 6th Assembly, Vancouver, in 1983, as her own German Protestant Church (EKD) and the evangelicals judged her far too radical! She had expected this from the evangelicals, because for thirty years they had hounded her as an infidel who should not be allowed to teach in the church. But she was surprised by this action of hr own Protestant church's council in Hanover. They claimed she was not representative and could not speak for the churches in West Germany. The EKD particularly disliked her widely quoted statement at that Assembly,

"Dear sisters and brothers, I speak to you as a woman from one of the richest countries of the earth, a country with a bloody history that reeks of gas, a history some of us Germans have not been able to forget; I come from a country that today holds the greatest concentration of atomic weapons in the world, ready for use."[16] The reaction was swift in West Germany, "How dare you foul the nest—why don't you go to East Germany?"[17] Besides the hate mail there were very fine letters of solidarity, particularly from women. So she did speak for a wide range of Christians. By dint of perseverance and tactics that shall remain undisclosed, we finally did get her on the podium—this small, slight person, with a sharp mind and a soaring generous spirit.

She refused to separate prayer and politics. Beginning with her girlhood in Nazi Germany, she engaged with the most pressing issues of our time—from the Holocaust to environmental justice. She always maintained that every theological statement must be a political statement as well. She took a stand in the controversial area of church and politics, and suffered for it. She was well versed in the thinking of theologian Paul Tillich, "a vocal opponent of the Nazis who in 1933 became the first non-Jewish professor to be barred from German universities and soon went into exile. Tillich…taught that the role of the church was in society, that the depth of its commitment and faith were measured by its engagement with politics and culture. It was this engagement that alone gave faith its vibrancy and worth."[18]

Dorothee was intensely interested in what it meant to be converted to Christ. She knew that her church in Nazi Germany justified National Socialism on misinterpreted Christian tradition. She wondered out loud why those nice German people, who played the violin and cello and read Goethe, tolerated what was going on. She pondered how the people who gassed others in Auschwitz and then went home and listened to Beethoven did this with no problem. She was an upper middle-class, liberal German girl who became a widely read poet and a radical Christian.

She was a pacifist and a feminist in a country that embraced neither at that time in its history. She longed for the old order to pass away, and endured a lot of pain, crying and ostracism because of her theological posture. She enjoyed the friendship of the radical Catholic pacifist Berrigan brothers, Daniel and

---

16 Dorothee Sölle, *Against the Wind*, p. 93.
17 Dorothee Sölle, *Against the Wind*, p. 93.
18 Chris Hedges, *American Fascists* (Free Press, NY: 2006), p. 195.

Philip, who worked against arms production during the Vietnam War. For her acts of solidarity with peace activists and her civil disobedience action on 6 Aug. 1985, Hiroshima Day, outside the Pershing II nuclear missile base in Fischbach, Germany, Dorothee was found guilty of "provoking arrest." Later in 1988, for a sit-down action for peace outside the gates of the US poison gas depot at Waldfischbach, Germany, she was found guilty of "attempting to provoke arrest." She writes, "Being arrested, criminalized, tried, and sentenced were important events in my life. They not only produced publicity but also bonded together all blockaders, young and old, prominent and unknown."[19]

> *Then I saw a new heaven and a new earth, for the first heaven and the first earth had vanished, and there was no longer any sea. I saw the holy city, new Jerusalem, coming down out of heaven from God, made ready like a bride adorned for her husband. I heard a loud voice proclaiming from the throne: "Now at last God has his dwelling among men! He will dwell among them and they shall be his people, and God himself will be with them. He will wipe every tear from their eyes; there shall be an end to death, and to mourning and crying and pain; for the old order has passed away!" Then he who sat on the throne said, "Behold! I am making all things new!"* (Revelation 21.1–5 NEB)

This text, read at her funeral, was so appropriate for this woman who was shunned by her own church, pilloried and denied academic place at the Faculty of Protestant Theology at the University of Mainz because her unorthodox approaches never conformed to the theology of the church.

Bishop Bärbel von Wartenberg-Potter, an ecumenical colleague who preached at Dorothee's funeral, had this to say about this text and its implications for us.

> "She longed for authentic encounter with God who speaks strongly to our self-centered and merciless time. A new heaven and a new earth is what John, exiled on Patmos, describes in his great vision of the book of Revelation. It is a vision of a new earth, differently constituted to the one we are used to, with a different way of living and thinking, a new way of loving, acting, and sharing. Our old earth is terribly drenched in

---

19 Dorothee Sölle, *Against the Wind*, p. 119.

blood, torn by war, and damaged by dying forests and withering fields. On our old earth, child soldiers in Africa learn to kill with easy-to-use and easily available guns made in Europe. Here wars are waged with fantastic precision...and hasten the breakdown of international law. On this earth, the unheeded cries of children, whose mothers have no bread to give them, die inaudibly...near the end of our text from Revelation, there is this promise, "Death shall be no more, mourning and crying and pain shall be no more." Dorothee's life confirmed the Easter structure of human existence, which transforms the mourning of abandonment into a cry of indignation, and the mourning of death into the quietness and certainty of nearness to God..."Everything carries on: that's what death is about," she remarked. Love carries on; praying and doing justice carry on. Bread is still baked. Children are conceived and born. The grain of wheat will fall into the soil and grow in the field, and in the heart of humans... we trust in the word of Revelation, "Behold! I make all things new!"

This vision of the end times reaches far beyond one's own death and puny efforts in one's life. It is so different from other apocalyptic visions found in the Bible, such as in Mark 13 and 2 Thessalonians 2, which emphasize vengeance and punishment of the wicked and rewards for the faithful only.

For many of our current faith community the passage holds out a vision of the end and goal of all our seeking—a vision of the proposed world which informs the everyday world in which we live. It is the world of Jesus: where compassion, justice, love, forgiveness and mercy are the reality. It is not just a hopeful mirage of the future, but exists richly and fully in the present wherever justice is realized, or compassion offered and accepted, or forgiveness accomplished. "Now at last God has his dwelling among us...I am making all things new." Such a vision is far more than the broken, well-intentioned but unsuccessful efforts of our own lives to seek justice and comfort for all defrauded of their lives. The vision here is communal, and is in continuity with God's work of justice we experience in this life. It is one of the city of the new Jerusalem, rising out of the death, mourning, crying and pain of people's lives.

Later in the chapter we have the wonderful vision of the Open City, whose gates will never be shut day or night. This passage was set to music for the opening worship of the sixth Assembly of the World Council of Churches, Vancouver, 1983, at which Dorothee Sölle spoke of the new heaven and new earth we so sorely need. Then Chapter 22.2 speaks of the "tree of life, which yields twelve crops of fruit...the leaves of the trees serve for the healing of the nations." This passage is in continuity with the work of God as healer in the Hebrew Bible, where we read of God's capacity to "make new" persons, nations, and all of creation which has been so distressingly distorted.

Dorothee Sölle knew that everything carries on; that's what death is about. Love carries on and making justice carries on. The grain of wheat falls into the soil, absorbs the nutrients of the soil around it, and then sprouts up with quite a different shape or body. There is both continuity and discontinuity.

John's vision of a new order of things is communal—a New Jerusalem. Governance is different. It is for the common good. Where have you seen this vision, or even a part of it, become a present reality? Where have you noticed God making "all things new?" In your family? In your society? Your country? In which parts of creation/the biosphere?

Frances (Frankie) Tillman, Canada

5 December 1916 – 8 October 2003

Unconventional Christian; Ecumenist; Feminist; critic and tireless activist; Indefatigable worker in YWCA; Teacher of Scripture at Balmoral Hall for Girls, Winnipeg; Lifelong member United Church of Canada. Married to Bob, three children, grandchildren.

I will never forget driving down Jarvis Street in Toronto at 2:00 am one morning and my car quit. Frankie immediately launched herself into the dark street and picked up a man. He who may have thought he was in for a good time with a prostitute ended up fixing my car!

I first met Frankie in 1957 when she and her husband Bob arrived in Winnipeg to enable him to assume the post of Dean of Theology of United College (now University of Winnipeg) until 1968. They had come directly from Geneva, Switzerland and she was full of ecumenical stories from around the world. I had never been out of Canada, and she found me "hopelessly" United Church and narrow in my outlook. I found her lively and provocative but tied up almost completely with her beloved YWCA. It was the basis for a long friendship as we expanded each other's horizons.

Our shared Winnipeg days were full of her task as "Scripture Mistress" (as my husband Roy designated her) at Balmoral private school for girls. This is where she brought the Bible alive for countless young women. She displayed a strong non-judgmental streak as she supported lesbians before it was acceptable to do so. I experienced her generous hospitality in Winnipeg, Calgary, and Vancouver, where cups of mulled wine were always waiting to welcome the visitor on a wintry day. She worked tirelessly and generously with street women in Vancouver's East side. I shared vicariously with her during her trip to Africa in the 1970s on behalf of the International YWCA, and her successful efforts to retain the "C" in YWCA. Some thought by removing the "C," standing for Christian, more money and people would be attracted to the Y. All of her efforts prompted the Vancouver Y to recognize her as a Woman of Distinction. Her faith was a central part of her life, and we had many a discussion on what it meant in our lives and in the lives of our children and friends and women of the East side—no holds barred. The first text is entirely appropriate for one who enjoyed life to the full and overflowed with vitality and goodwill.

> *I summon heaven and earth to witness against you this day: I offer you the choice of life or death, blessing or curse. Choose life and then you and your descendants will live; love the Lord your God, obey him and hold fast to him; that is life for you and length of days in the land which the Lord swore to give to your forefathers, Abraham, Isaac, and Jacob.*
>
> (Deuteronomy 30.19–20 NEB)

How appropriate for Frankie, who struggled with intermittent depression in her later years, but knew scripture that recalled for her the promises, acts, and gifts of God through the ages and for her as well. There was no amnesia in her faith journey, but rather a strong remembrance of its narrative and its admonition to 'obey and hold fast' and the reassurance that her life choices would bring life and blessing, or death and curses. She chose life!

I will not easily forget a dinner she hosted in her Vancouver home for women from around the world who attended "The Well," a meeting place at the 1983 World Council of Churches 6th Assembly in Vancouver. "The Well" had been established to ensure that female delegates as well as female visitors from around the world would have a space to engage with and hear each other, since the Assembly was predominately male. Suddenly, outside, we heard glorious music. The Russian Orthodox female ensemble had decided to take their singings outdoors to her backyard. All the windows and doors of the neighbourhood popped open to hear what was going on in their back lane. Choose life indeed! What a woman. "But if the while I think on thee dear friend, / All losses are restor'd and sorrows end."[20]

Here is another text used at her funeral.

> *"Who will separate us from the love of Christ? Will hardship, or distress, or persecution, or nakedness, or peril, or sword? ... No in all these things we are more than conquerors through him who loved us. For I am convinced that neither death, nor life, nor angels, nor rulers, nor things present nor things to come, nor powers, nor height, nor depth, nor anything else in all creation, will be able to separate us from the love of God in Christ Jesus our Lord."*
>
> (Romans 8.37–39 NRSV)

So nothing can separate us from the love of God in Christ? Neither depression nor anxiety, shame nor alienation, marginalization nor persecution, despair nor apathy, dictatorial rulers nor refugee status for life, success nor failure can separate us from the love of God. Can this be true?

The text drives us back to consider the Easter claim that has not been taken seriously or given credibility in our affluent, self-sufficient society. Some of us are comfortable in our life style. Who then needs God? But who of us has not known failure, depression, or distress in our dysfunctional families? Who of us has reached the top rung of our profession, only to face emptiness and a sense of "what now?" Who of us is afraid of admitting our own vulnerability? Who among us hasn't enough to eat? Who among us has far too much to eat, but whose life is bereft of meaning? Who of us are refugees, having known "persecution, nakedness, peril, and sword," but still face a most uncertain future? Who of us are crammed into prison cells or suffering mental health problems?

The Easter affirmation is that nothing can separate us from the love of God. Life is stronger than death; love is stronger than hate; forgiveness is stronger than vengeance. It is about the transforming power of life given by the sovereignty of God—an ongoing process. It is about rejecting the power of death and despair currently embraced in today's world, by choosing life. It is about the advent of a new regime of compassion, justice and love. But does it hold water?

---

20 William Shakespeare, *Sonnet XXX* in *The Complete Works* (NY: Gramercy Books, 1975), p. 1196.

I keep meeting resurrected people who have chosen life. Frankie was one of them. Another one is my long-time friend who has spent a lifetime recovering from sexual abuse. She wrote me, "I was uncertain about embracing Christianity whole hog. Life was not as simple as it said. It doesn't happen like a Walt Disney movie where it all ends up happy. It's hard, though there is relief. Choose. So I chose and vacillated. Chose again and vacillated. These days, in tough times I simply say to myself, choose life." On another occasion she wrote, "Prayer is just saying thank you, thank you, thank you twenty times. I was dead and now I am alive."

After a World Council of Churches' consultation in Cyprus, we all went out to eat and dance and have fun to celebrate the completion of our work. When the dancing started I noticed that the man sitting next to me was not getting up to dance. He was a doctor from Zaire. When I asked him if he was not going to dance, he told me that his church didn't allow it. A number of churches worldwide continue to ban dancing, as it is regarded as the first step on the slippery slope to sexual encounters. It is only two or three generations ago that Methodists in Canada advocated for this position. I responded to my friend by saying I thought he should read the Bible more, as there were a number of instances of dancing in it, and besides, wouldn't he like to learn how to dance? His eyes lit up, and we made our way to the dance floor. I am no great dance teacher, as my husband Roy used to tell me, but we managed. Our dance was not a graceful waltz, nor a fast fox trot. I am sure it was not beautiful to watch. It was awkward and tentative, just like our lives as Christians. But we were dancing! And the smile that gradually lit up that man's face was electrifying. Resurrection is sometimes the difference between sitting morosely and dancing with abandon. Frankie would have loved that man.

Our dance was a metaphor for the church today. It represented the difference between congregational members sitting in the "comfortable pew" written of by journalist Pierre Berton a few decades ago, in contrast to living a life unafraid of risks, or error, or failure, or embarrassment as we, the church, try new things. Our steps may also be tentative because we are afraid. What is important is that we get up and try.

K.H. Ting (Ting Kuang-hsun), China

20 September 1915 – 22 November 2012

Patriotic religious and ecumenical leader; Anglican priest and then Bishop ('42–'50); and Mission Secretary to Canadian Student Christian Movement ('46); Post graduate at Columbia and Union Theological Seminary, NY; Sec. of World Student Christian Federation, Geneva ('48–'51); Returned to Mao's China ('51) and held three positions: Chair of Three Self Movement of Protestants (Self-Governing; Aelf-Supporting; Self-Propagating); President China Christian Council; President Nanjing Union Theological Seminary; later a Founder of Amity that printed and distributed Bibles in China ('85) Vice Chair of the Chinese People's Political Consultative Conference ('89–'08); K.H. and his wife Siu May both given honorary degrees from Emmanuel College, Toronto ('89); Delegate to National People's Congress (China's legislature). Married to Siu May, two children.

"I was assigned for a short time to building the Nanjing Yangtze River Bridge," said K.H. Ting with a twinkle in his eye, speaking to me of his role in the Cultural Revolution of '66–'76. "I wasn't very good at hitting nails on the head." Churches had been vandalized by Red Guards and converted to secular use; Christians like K.H. had been expelled from their homes (all their possessions including his theological library, seized). All seminaries had been closed, and at the height of the Revolution, not a single Christian church remained open in the whole of China.

I first met K.H. Ting in Winnipeg in 1946, when he visited for a week as part of a cross Canada tour of Student Christian Movement groups in Canadian Universities. At the time, I was active in the Manitoba SCM and got to squire this handsome man around to some of our meetings. He was then World Mission Secretary for the movement, charged with educating students about the role of Christian mission in the world. Many in the church then, as now, thought that mission meant duplicating ourselves and making more converts. Very few criticized this understanding. He was the first person who pointed out to me that we Christians are called to be salt and yeast—they are very small substances, but it is absolutely mandatory that they function! So mission was not to be understood as multiplying salt or leaven, or necessarily increasing the fold by huge numbers, but rather giving flavour to the society, and allowing the yeast of the gospel to create and permeate a new society.

I remember him particularly because he urged upon me the double role of mother and working woman, in the post-war context of "married women should stay home and not work." He told me that most women in China (including his wife) maintained a home and family but also worked outside the home. Why didn't I? I had had very affirming experiences as student minister on rural summer four point "mission fields" in Manitoba in 1944–45, and had written my parents that I was thinking of ordination. But it took me some time to internalize this idea, which was counter-cultural at that time. I had put this question to the back of my mind, and didn't re-examine it again until I met K.H. Ting.

In 1950, at the time of Mao's revolution, K.H.'s friends urged him not to return to China, because they equated atheistic Marxism with a strong anti-Christian bias. He would not be safe. But for K.H., who was unmistakably Christian and fully Chinese, it meant strong support for the struggle of the Chinese people, and his effective attempt to contextualize the gospel in China. He became Chair of the Three Self Movement that espouses self-propagating, self-supporting, and self-governing churches in China, independently from Western support. He also helped found the Nanjing Theological Seminary. Having been a founding members of the WCC in 1948, China ended official participation in 1956 in protest at the West's role in siding with the "colonizers" in the Korean war. Significantly, it was the Canadian churches who, in 1981, were invited by K.H. to "make a new beginning" and heal the wounds of history. It was K.H. Ting who, at the WCC Canberra Assembly of 1991, steered the Chinese Christian Council back into membership in the WCC.

K.H told me that in a curious way, the subsequently discredited Cultural Revolution that rocked China in the '66-'76 decade brought Christians of his persuasion into the mainstream of Chinese society. Communist party members, whose main experience with Western Christians up to that point had been with those fixated on individual salvation and deliverance from this evil world, now became aware of Christians who were concerned not only with personal salvation but also with the social fabric of society. Party members began to see that religion was not necessarily the opiate of the people.

We know that there are various ways of speaking about the resurrection in the Bible. There is Paul's belief in continuity and transformation of the individual into a "spiritual body," as in John 11.22-27 as well as in 1 Corinthians 15. There is also the promise of a new governance and a transformed community, as is envisioned in Isaiah 25.6-9, as well as the "new heaven and the new earth" of Revelation 21.1-4. Both the John and the Isaiah passages were read at his funeral and point to K.H. embracing both the personal and the communal promises of the resurrection. His gospel emphasis was always personal, but not individualistic, as one finds in evangelistic churches in China.

His funeral text is singularly appropriate for him.

> *On this mountain the Lord of Hosts will prepare a banquet of rich fare for all the peoples, a banquet of wines well matured and richest fare, well-matured wines strained clear. On this mountain the Lord will swallow up that veil that shrouds all the peoples, the pall thrown over the nations; he will swallow up death for forever. Then the Lord God will wipe away the tears from every face and remove the reproach of his people from the whole earth. The Lord has spoken.*
> (Isaiah 25.6-9 NEB)

Here is a text for a new community and for the intended world that can inform our everyday world. The previous verses have recorded the city as being a ruin, a heap, the palace of aliens, a city no more," full of refugees and of the needy and of the ruthless" (Isaiah 25.2-5, NRSV). How contemporary! Think of the thousands of refugees fleeing Sudan or the Congo, and of the ruthless people that have brought about this situation. Think of the needy folk without hope or a future.

The prophet Isaiah proposes an alternate story. His poetry envisions hope and healing for the inhabitants of destroyed cities and ruined dreams:,like to the Messianic banquet, which will be a feast of fat things and the finest wine, transparency between nations, and comfort for the suffering ones. How appropriate for K.H. who lived in a country struggling to feed its citizens; practicing strict censorship rules; striving to lift its millions of suffering people into a new day. While respecting Confucianism and Buddhism which were extant in China, he spent his life helping resurrect the Christian community in China. It is clear to me that for him, resurrection had a strong communal dimension, as well as personal, and had to do with the fabric of societal life in his vast country. It had to do with communities that stand up for justice, a roof over one's head, food for all, peace and understanding between peoples.

In the Eastern Orthodox Christian tradition, the icons present the vision of the Resurrection in communal terms. Jesus is never presented alone, but always in company with others who are being raised to new life with him. I saw these in Orthodox churches in Cyprus, Russia, Ethiopia, Crete, Greece, and Turkey. These strong images are in closer continuity with the Jewish idea of the redeemed community and the new governance in Isaiah than Western individualistic images that emphasize Jesus resurrected alone. Why did the West ever give up the Eastern vision? Surely the East and the West complement each other in this matter.

What does this mean for the faith community? The strong metaphor used in the poetry of this passage is clearly saying that God's reign is already begun here among us. God's intentions are beginning to be realized, and we are "the first fruits of them that slept" (1 Corinthians 15.20 KJV). We are a resurrected people in so far as we have chosen to reject the unjust values that prevailed in the Roman Empire and continue to prevail in current "empires." The resurrection continues in so far as our lives are conformed to God's intention in our daily choices in this world.

We the living, who faithfully try to live God's intention for our lives and for the world, are in continuity with those who have faithfully gone before us and have died. We call them the "communion of saints" and I have often heard them clapping and urging us on. I know K.H. is one of them.

Chapter 3
Transformation

Ruth Nita Barrow, Barbados
November 1916 – 19 December 1995

Adult educator; Nurse and health care activist; feminist Methodist; Public health administrator Jamaica and Barbados ('40–'50); Studied nursing at University of Toronto ('44–'48), Edinburgh and Columbia University; World President of various groups: YWCA ('75–'83): International Council of Adult Education ('82–'90); World Council of Churches ('83–'91); Director of WCC Christian Medical Commission ('71–'81); Convener of NGO Forum for Women at UN Congress of Women in Nairobi ('95); Barbados Ambassador to United Nations ('86–'90); Member Commonwealth Group of Eminent Persons visiting South Africa ('86); Governor General of Barbados ('90–'95). Made Dame of British Empire ('80).

"Only tourists have time to drink coconut juice," the speaker was saying. She was a large black woman, Nita Barrow by name, who was addressing church delegates from around the world in Geneva in 1972 at the offices of the World Council of Churches. A feisty Methodist from Barbados ("platinum coast to Canadian retirees"), she was talking about the Caribbean as the "sugar bowl of Europe," and of Henry Morgan, a rum rascal who had exploited the sugar rich islands, and was subsequently invited to England and knighted!

Although she was Governor General of Barbados, she lived in a small house on a hill which afforded her a panoramic view of the endless ocean. One night when I was watching TV with her, the picture faded, and she banged the set, only to have the picture restored. It would never have occurred to her to buy a new TV. She was modest in her lifestyle and yet exuded the air and presence of a distinguished person. She delighted in attending the small Methodist church in Bridgetown which had nurtured her faith over many years. She is one of the few women I know who could "hold court" and pull it off with complete aplomb. She became a good friend, and Roy and I visited her in New York when she was Barbadian Ambassador to the United Nations ('86–'90) and when Stephen Lewis mobilized support (unsuccessfully) to try to make her the first female President of the General Assembly of the United Nations.

I have chosen two texts that are appropriate for her life, given the fact that she was both a nation builder and a midwife.

> *Shall a woman bear a child without pains? give birth to a son before the onset of labour? Who has heard of anything like this? Who has seen any such thing? Shall a country be born after one day's labour, shall a nation be brought to birth all in a moment? But Zion, at the onset of her pangs, bore her sons. Shall I bring to the point of birth and not deliver? The Lord says; shall I who deliver close the womb?*
> (Isaiah 66.7–9 NEB)

Verses 7–9 are saturated with birth language pointing to the radical power of God to bring about something completely new, though not without struggle and pain. The birth image (which signals fulfillment in Israel's story) contrasts so sharply with the old narratives of barrenness (which mean hopelessness, as in the story of Hannah, 1 Samuel 1–2.8 NEB).

Nita knew all about the struggles, pains, and joys of birthing a nation. She was fifty years of age when Barbados, a British colony since 1627, was finally granted its independence by an Act of Parliament of the UK. On 30 Nov. 1966, it became the fourth English-speaking country in the West Indies to achieve this. Years later, she was to become the first female Governor General of her country (1990–95). When Roy and I visited her in Barbados on that occasion, he was pleased to sleep in the same bed that Prince Philip had vacated a few days before! Being Governor General, however, was not all fun and games for her. The decision as to whether capital punishment applied to a particular prisoner was firmly in her hands alone. She was the final arbiter of justice in her country.

There is a text that speaks of justice and nation-building. Chapter 1 of

Exodus tells the story of the desperate situation of the Israelite slaves in Egypt, forced by Pharaoh into heavy labour and to "work on clay and brick-making, and all sorts of work in the fields" (Exodus 1.14 NEB). The new king was worried, because the Israelite population continued to increase in numbers, and "they will become masters of the country" (Exodus 1.10 NEB).

> *Then the king of Egypt spoke to the Hebrew midwives, whose names were Shiprah and Puah. "When you are attending the Hebrew women in child birth," he told them, "watch as the child is delivered and it is a boy, kill him; and if it is a girl let her live." But they were God-fearing women. They did not do what the king of Egypt had told them to do, but let the boys live. Pharaoh summoned the Hebrew midwives and asked them why they had done this and let the boys live. They told Pharaoh that Hebrew women were not like Egyptian women. When they were in labour they gave birth before the midwife could get to them. So...the people increased in numbers...Pharaoh then ordered all his people to throw every new-born Hebrew boy into the Nile ,but to let the girls live.*
>
> (Exodus 1:15–22 NEB)

This is one of the first Biblical stories to tell the astonishing, stunning role of women in nation-building. The imperative of justice is achieved through the subversive words and acts of seemingly innocent midwives. It astounds me that Pharaoh fell for the midwives' explanation hook, line and sinker. It surprises me even more that they had the audacious courage to outwit him by their story. This text places justice for the oppressed firmly at the centre of nation-building for the people of God, in this case the Israelites. It endorses non-compliance with unjust authority. Ordinary midwives do it.

Nita was a midwife extraordinaire. She loved to tell the story of her work with the '85 United Nations World Congress on Women in Nairobi. As Convener of the Non-Government Organization (and as a former midwife who was used to facilitating something entirely new) she corralled the delegates from both Israel and Palestine, put them in a tent, and told them not to come out until they had come to some reasonable agreement about the future of their countries or she would knock their heads together. They did, and although their peace agreement never took effect, they forged personal solidarity ties that continued for years to come.

In 1990 Nita and I were dispatched to represent the World Council to the celebrations of Namibian independence from South Africa which took place in Windhoek, Namibia. Immediately she befriended the African women and was quite at home posing for photos with her black sisters from various African states. She had a gift for connecting grass roots folk with those in high government office, thereby bringing to birth a new relationship.

When she headed up the World Council of Churches' Medical Commission, she brought to birth for churches a concept of health that was understood far more broadly than medicine and recovery from diseases. She once invited me to a consultation on "The Congregation as Healing Community" to be held in Bali that fall. I had just been elected Moderator of the United Church, and to my regret the General Council staff thought I should not be racing off to Bali! She later had me attend a similar consultation in Cyprus, where I met healthcare providers and ministers from Guatemala, Zaire, New Zealand and many other points of the compass, co-operating in this important work. These were only the prelude to many other encounters and invitations from this remarkable woman.

She was an untiring advocate for women in civil society and Government circles. As she was the only female in the Commonwealth Group of Eminent Persons visiting South Africa in 1986, she thwarted the country's restrictions by entering the restricted area of Alexandria Township disguised in African garb and head dress as a seemingly innocent person.

It was at the WCC 1983 Vancouver Assembly she was elected one of its six Presidents. This happened not only because the Assembly had voted for "affirmative action" that guaranteed three out of six Presidents would be female. It was also because she had her finger on women's place in the member churches of the WCC, and was not slow to point out that women outnumbered men two to one in those churches, but men made all the policy decisions. Her election was recognition of her sterling record as an advocate of women, particularly through the YWCA, of which she had served as World President for eight years.

What implications do these texts on midwifery and nation building have for us? In what sense do you consider yourself a midwife, or a nation builder? Are you prepared for the hard labour involved in giving birth to a more just society in this country? How do you stand with the oppressed in our country? Are you able to recognize those who are victimized by unjust structures in which you may even be complicit? How many indigenous people do you know by name? How many incarcerated prisoners? Who are you working with to establish justice in this country? Who are your allies? What role does your congregation play?

Verna Isabel Margaret Freeman, Canada

4 January 1923 – 27 March 2002

> Musician; Private piano teacher; Choir director and accompanist; Music in worship; Piano duets for children and grandchildren. School teacher; United Church member; Active in Marriage Encounter; Talents as clown and palliative care worker; Amnesty supporter; Camper at Lake of the Woods and church camps; Bird watcher and wood carver; Specialized in hugs, winks and smiles. "Love is a decision" headed her obituary. Married to John, three children, four grandchildren. My sister-in-law.

"When the Saints Go Marching In" rocked the sanctuary as the funeral of my friend Ted Ockels came to a conclusion. Ted was a businessman as well as a jazz pianist and elder in the Presbyterian Church of Lafayette-Orinda, located near San Francisco, California. I met him while on a six-week stint as occupant of the Chair of Contemporary Theology at that church. It is to him I owe the idea for the title of this book. He wanted his entry into the next world to be celebrative! At funerals I have sung everything from "Shall We Gather at the River" to "Morning Has Broken" to "Bread and Roses" to "Lord of the Dance" to "Give Thanks for Life" to "Exsultate Jubilate." A book about the significance of music choices at funerals is just waiting to be written by some discerning soul.

My sister-in-law Margaret was quite right in insisting on the importance of the music chosen not only for funerals, but also for other occasions, because it is our hymns that carry the emotional freight and the spiritual depth of our faith. She was a musician, and her favourite hymn was "Spirit of God, Descend Upon my Heart" (VU #378), the first verse of which ends with "and make me love you as I ought to love." She also loved "Give to Us Laughter" (VU #624) and she thoroughly enjoyed introducing this hymn to congregations when it first appeared. She even had people at Regent Park United Church in Winnipeg float a balloon around during the singing of the hymn. She would have been a kindred spirit with Megumi Saunders of First Metropolitan United Church, Victoria, who recently had the children celebrate joy and laughter during the children's time in church, and had about one hundred helium balloons released from the gallery and everywhere else on the unsuspecting congregation. Soon we were all batting them back and forth to each other and having a wonderful time! Margaret would have loved that. And then there is Beethoven's grand music for "Joyful, Joyful We Adore You" (VU #232), which she loved. All of these hymns celebrated her joy in life and thanksgiving for the grace and blessing of simply being alive.

I knew Margaret well before my brother married her. She and I were in the same Arts year at United College (now the University of Winnipeg) and she majored in music. Her distinctive contribution was always music, although, to her credit, at age 65 she received her Masters degree in Educational Psychology. Musically it was either piano duets, accompanying choirs, facilitating sing songs, or just playing the piano for the joy of doing it! No wonder, then, that the music chosen for her funeral was more important to her than the scripture. But it is not a surprise to discover that the following passage of scripture read at her funeral reflected her joy in life:

> *but those who wait for the Lord shall renew their strength, they shall mount up with wings like eagles, they shall run and not be weary, they shall walk and not faint.*
> (Isaiah 40.31 NRSV)

Renewal will come in God's good time. It cannot be summoned by more busyness or more committee meetings. It will come only as we open our hearts and spirits to the Creator who gives us life. This speaks to the necessity of regular withdrawal from furious activity for the committed person, and the imperative of meditation. The prophet speaks of how God comes to those who wait, particularly those with feelings of despair or spiritual exhaustion. And who of us has not been in that number from time to time?

Margaret's conviction was that love was not just a sentimental feeling. The phrase her children chose to highlight at her funeral was a phrase from her Marriage Encounter Work, "love is a decision." Margaret knew this, and affirmed it in her work with that program that facilitated healthy relationships between marriage partners. Much depended on the self-understanding each partner had of "love." Margaret claimed that love is an act of will, not a feeling, and the following text, read at her funeral, bears her out.

> *If I speak in the tongues of mortals and of angels, but do not have love, I am a noisy gong or a clanging symbol. And if I have prophetic powers, and understand all mysteries and all knowledge, and if I have all faith, so as to remove mountains, but do not have love, I am nothing. If I give away all my possessions, and I hand over my body so that I may boast, but do not have love, I gain nothing. Love is patient; love is kind; love is not envious or boastful or arrogant or rude. It does not insist on its own way; it is not irritable or resentful; it does not rejoice in wrongdoing, but rejoices in the truth. It bears all things, believes all things, hopes all things, endures all things. Love never ends...For now we see in a mirror dimly, but then we will see face to face. Now I know only in part; then I will know fully, even as I have been fully known. And now faith, hope, and love abide, these three; and the greatest of these is love.* (1 Corinthians 13.1-8, 12-13 NRSV)

This used to be a favourite text to be read at weddings, because it is a realistic "take" on the nature of love. Perhaps that is why it is so commonly overlooked now in favour of a sentimental love poem that the prospective bride has picked out of a current magazine. The text is a great antidote to the current pop idea of love, tied exclusively to sex, that is rampant in our culture. The Biblical text is also about the grittiness of human relationships rather than sentimental feelings. My mother used to say, "Don't marry a man unless you are comfortable washing his dirty socks." This text is not the "eros" or erotic love spoken of in Song of Songs, and addressed elsewhere in this book. This is "agape," a self-giving relationship with another.

I especially like the second paragraph that describes love as patient, kind, not envious or boastful or rude or resentful, and not insisting on its own way. Who of us can claim to have shown that kind of love to another? Yet is it not realistic and absolutely necessary to maintain and nurture any intimate relationship?

When I was Ecumenist in Residence at Toronto School of Theology, I had access to seven denominational schools of Theology, including Presbyterian, United Church, Anglican (high and low!) and Roman Catholic. Church history and doctrinal differences forbade us celebrating the Lord's Supper together, so instead, at the beginning of the University term, we would gather for an "Agape Meal" or Love Feast together. Here we freely shared wine and food, thoughts and doubts, disappointments and successes. It had nothing to do with sex and everything to do with authentic human relationships and the nature of love. It was based on New Testament practice documented in the Book of Acts.

After Pentecost,

> *All who believed were together and had all things in common; they would sell their possessions and goods and distribute the proceeds to all, as any had need. Day by day, as they spent much time together in the temple, they broke bread at home and ate their food with glad and generous hearts, praising God and having the goodwill of all the people.* (Acts 2:44–47 NRSV)

Shortly after my husband Roy died, I received a note from Robin McLaren, who had been a young teenage girl in 1980, when I was elected Moderator of the United Church of Canada. A member of our congregation in Hamilton at the time, she wrote to say that she had watched my installation on television, with Roy fully present on the podium, and that she had never seen a man as proud of another person as Roy obviously was with me at that moment. Indeed, he continued to show that love and support all through the ensuing years, claiming that he, as Prince Philip did with the Queen, walked four steps behind me. I noticed that as time went on, he shortened it to one step! But he was never envious, always supportive, and Robin noticed the loving support.

A close friend, Dorothy Wyman, wrote this short obituary for her husband Harold (see p. 173 of this book) when he died. "Devoted husband and father; faithful pastor; generous companion and friend; a good and gentle man." Nothing of his many accomplishments, his education, his honours, his faithful services to his church. She might also have added that he was a loving person. "And the greatest of these is love." Margaret also knew this.

KATHERINE BOEHNER HOCKIN, CANADA-CHINA

1910–1993

Missionary educator; Daughter of missionary parents; Born and raised in China; Higher education in Canada; One of first female students at Emmanuel College, Toronto; Sponsored by Women's Missionary Society (WMS) to study for Doctorate in Theology in India; Taught at Ahousat, Vancouver Island Residential school; United Church Training School Toronto; With Student Christian Movement in China; Dean of Studies and Librarian at Canadian School of Missions and the Ecumenical Institute. She taught the evolution of missiology and its ecumenical dimensions to an entire generation and to all denominations. Wrote "Servants of God in People's China" ('62); "Katharine Hockin Lane" named in her honour by the City of Toronto ('13).

I was surprised when she loaned me her handwritten "India diary." Rather than study for her theological PhD in Canada, she had chosen to go to India and immerse herself in the thinking and practices of Asia. I should not have been surprised, because she was an unconventional woman. She rode her bike everywhere in Toronto, even in her eightieth year. She always took her knitting to Toronto Presbytery meetings but was totally aware of proceedings at all times. Even her knitting had purpose, as it was not unusual to find that she was crafting a shawl for Korean women, suffering persecution under a dictatorship. She moved students beyond the traditional understanding of mission as "sending" to forging mutual relations of partners working together ecumenically as companions. Even the neighbourhood and city where she lived recognized her uniqueness. How many missionaries have the City of Toronto name a lane after them as was done for her twenty years after her death?

Born in China of missionary parents, she had first-hand experience as a missionary in China until she left in 1950 when missionaries became *personae non gratae* due to the state of war existing between U.S.A. and Chinese troops over North Korea. She continued to have an abiding interest in all things Chinese, and particularly of the emerging indigenous Protestant Church of Christ in China based on the Three Self Movement: Self-Governing; Self-Supporting, Self-Propagating.[1] It emerged with strength after the revolution as an indigenous expression of Christianity validating Chinese culture, supporting the People's Republic of China but remaining committed to Jesus Christ. When I visited China I noted that the China Christian Council, based on the Three Self Movement, allowed and affirmed sacramental practices of all the former Western denominations. Baptism could be for infants or believers; Communion could be wine or grape juice; all former practices were welcomed in the post-denominational church.

Her greatest contribution was the wedding of ecumenism and mission in new ways, and making that understanding clear to several generations of both Protestants and Catholics. She was fully aware of all themes taken at the large global Protestant Missionary Conferences held every decade, although she never attended any of them. She studied the documents coming out of those meetings, and summarized the main thrusts of a given decade for her students. She spoke with ease about the largely Western delegations attending the 1910 Edinburgh Conference with its theme, "the evangelization of the world in this generation." She would then go on to detail further conferences such as Madras 1938 where the provisional committee forming the World Council of Churches was formed.

If she had lived, she would have spoken of the more recent ones, such as 2005 Athens, attended for the first time by a Chinese delegation and of a broad representation of Pentecostals and evangelicals; Boston 2010, which considered the implications of the 100th anniversary of the 1910 Edinburgh conference; and Manila 2012, with its understanding of evangelism in a world of religious plurality.

At her funeral, her prayer shawls bedecked the sanctuary and the following text was read,

---
1 See the entry for K.H. Ting on page 91 of this book.

> *I appeal to Evodia and I appeal to Syntyche to come to agreement with each other, in the Lord; and I ask you, Syzygus, to be truly a "companion" and to help them in this. These women were a help to me when I was fighting to defend the Good News... Let your tolerance be evident to everyone; the Lord is very near....Keep doing all the things that you learned from me and have been taught by me and have heard or seen that I do...* (Philippians 4.2-3, 5, 9, Jerusalem Bible)

"Companion" is the meaning of the proper name Syzgus and it was a term introduced into any talk of mission by Katharine. She abandoned words such as missionary or fraternal worker or even partner, because she believed that walking with the "other" in companionship was a more authentic way of expressing contemporary Christian convictions about relationships. It is instructive also to note that the text speaks openly of a disagreement and the mutual dependence of the women. Katharine was always a team player, recognizing the mutual supportive roles women played in the church, having learned this as she worked with her companions in China.

"Keep doing all these things you have learned from me and have been taught by me" (Philippians 4.9 Jerusalem Bible). The Canadian School of Mission where Katharine taught for many years was birthed in 1917 by representatives of the Mission Boards of the mainline churches, as well as the theological colleges at University of Toronto. It developed many functions over the years: linguistics for those preparing to go overseas; courses for missionaries on furlough; orientation for those preparing themselves for mission work; tutoring; developing a specialized library; and hosting Memorial lectures in the name of the founder of the School, L.Lowell Murray, that brought such luminaries as José Miguez Bonino of Argentina and M.M. Thomas of India (see p. 54 and p. 169 of this book) to the campus. Katherine worked and taught issues of justice in global engagement and encounters between cultures and faiths for over fifty years at what was later to become the Ecumenical Institute as part of a staff team, and told me frequently that the glue that held them together in solidarity was the daily worship they enjoyed.

The last part of the text is singularly appropriate for her as well:

> *I have learned to manage on whatever I have. I know how to be poor and I know how to be rich too. I have been through my initiation and now I am ready for anything anywhere: full stomach or empty stomach, poverty or plenty. There is*

nothing I cannot master with the help of the One who gives me strength.
(Philippians 4.11b-14 Jerusalem Bible)

In her years in China before Mao's revolution she would have seen full stomach and empty stomach, both poverty and plenty, and known that when there was no shared companionship along the way, revolution was the inevitable result of such disparities.

In a similar vein is the Isaiah 65.17-25 NEB text read at her funeral. It speaks a vision of a transformed society—the new Jerusalem—that has been so beautifully illustrated in the lino cut on page 104 of this book.

For behold, I create new heavens and a new earth. Former things shall no longer be remembered, nor shall they be called to mind. Rejoice and be filled with delight, you boundless realms which I create; for I create Jerusalem to be a delight, and her people a joy. I will take delight in Jerusalem and rejoice in my people; weeping and cries for help shall never again be heard in her. There no child shall ever again die an infant, no old man fail to live out his life; every boy shall live his hundred years before he dies, whoever falls short of a hundred shall be despised. Men shall build houses and live to inhabit them, plant vineyards and eat their fruit; they shall not build for others to inhabit nor plant for others to eat. My people shall live the long life of a tree....They shall not toil in vain or raise children for misfortune.... The wolf and the lamb shall feed together and the lion shall eat straw like cattle. They shall not hurt or destroy in all my holy mountain, says the Lord.

Here is a marvelous vision of newness and hope for a people who live in despair, especially the despair of exile.

The new city will exhibit justice between people, peace and wholeness in its social relationships. Infant mortality will be low; old age will be honoured and supported. Economic security will exist as men build houses and do not risk losing them to invaders. Fertility of the soil will be restored. Abundant food will be available for all. There will be no more weeping and cries of despair will give way to hope. This is a vision that invites singing and dancing. It is also a vision that invites public practice of the human relationships envisioned.

Katherine Hockin's life was a living out of that vision. Her question to us, I think, would be: "How does one keep open the possibility of full companionship so that the 'new Jerusalem' can arise concretely in our midst?"

Mary Coyne Rowell Jackman, Canada
7 January 1904 – July 1994

Advocate of social and political change; Feminist; Methodist and later United Church; Founder of Women's branch of Canadian Institute of International Affairs; Sec. Student Christian Movement, University of Toronto (U of T) ('26–'29;) nationalist and internationalist; Philanthropist; ecumenist; patron of Arts; London School of Economics; YWCA, Selley Oaks, UK; Member Victoria College Senate, Board of Governors (U of T); Established Polyani Chair in Chemistry (U of T). Married to Henry, four children.

There is an apocryphal story that Tim Buck, Leader of the Communist party of Canada, alleged to owe the one vote he received in the Rosedale riding of Toronto to Mary Jackman. I wished I had known her earlier in my life. I met her only in the mid 1970s when we moved to Southern Ontario from Thunder Bay. She was then in her sixties.

When I learned that she had been a student delegate to several European conferences of the Student Christian Movement and then the SCM secretary at the University of Toronto (1928–29), I knew that I shared her commitment to social justice. She had a lively interest in current affairs, demonstrated by her founding a women's branch of the Canadian Institute for International Affairs after she discovered that women had been excluded from meetings in Hart House at the University of Toronto. She acquired knowledge of the world and its politics through her father, a 1921 delegate to the League of Nations, and a round-the-world tour in 1925 with her family's missionary and government friends and judges. From that privileged background she delivered a life committed to the welfare of others, particularly women.

She would do anything to support women, and she came by it honestly. Her mother, Nell Langford, graduated from Victoria College, University of Toronto in 1896 and was active in political life, in such women's movements as the YWCA, and in co-founding the Ontario Women's Liberal Association. Her aunt Mary Rowell was the first woman professor at Victoria College. I had known of the fame of her father, Newton Rowell, a lawyer and Methodist lay preacher, who won the famous "person's case" in 1929, establishing for the first time that all Canadian women are legally persons under the British North America Act and therefore eligible to sit in the Senate. When I had occasion to research the archives at the E.J. Pratt Library at Victoria College, I was proudly shown the world's best collection of hand-printed books by the Bloomsbury group, a collection begun by Mary when her mother gave her a copy of Virginia Woolf's *A Room of One's Own* on her 1929 engagement to Harry. Is it any wonder that Mary Jackman was a strong advocate for women's education and that Victoria College has the Rowell-Jackman Residence, so students could have a room of their own?

In 1992, when she received an honorary L.L.D. degree from the University of Toronto, she said, "I am a woman who stands at the midpoint of three generations of women who have cared deeply about what was called, sixty years ago, 'the social gospel.' It represented a belief that religion was not a private vision of God but a message about responsibility and concern for others…we seek a commitment in a nation, a world, where life is fair for everyone, where our children are fed and treasured, where there is safety and clean air, and no war. None of you should be satisfied with anything less."[2] She was 88 at the time. Wow!

What an antidote to those who practice religion as a private affair. Here is the testimony of a women firmly grounded in the prophetic Biblical tradition that advocated with Isaiah, "There no child shall ever again die an infant, no old man fail to live out his life" (Isaiah 65.20 NEB). In 1937 she founded the Bond Child Development Centre for children of workers on minimum income at Metropolitan United Church, Toronto which continues to this day.

---

2 Transcription of videotape of Mary Jackman's address to graduates at the University of Toronto (1992), given to me by her daughter, Senator Nancy Ruth.

In her late forties, she returned to the University to study art history, and this interest remained with her for the rest of her life. She did so because the colours and textures of painting spoke to her of the emotions in her life. She knew and supported artists such as Ann MacIntosh Duff, Rody Kenny Courtice, Sophia Buckingham, A.Y. Jackson and Wil Ogilvie. She hosted them at her Lake Huron cottage, and the works of art they painted (sometimes on the walls of that cottage) are now safely ensconced in the halls of the National Art Gallery in Ottawa. What a gift to Canada and other galleries across the nation.

I found this another fascinating linkage with my own life. At an exhibition of the paintings of Emily Carr in Victoria, BC a few years ago, I found myself moved to tears by the energy and love for life so evident in her painting "Juice of Life." It touched me emotionally at a deep level that surprised me. On my extensive international travels, the first place I sought out in a strange city was the Art Gallery. I knew that the foremost artists of a given country were like the canary in the mine—they would, in their paintings or sculptures, be the first ones to signal distress in a culture. The artists helped me understand the ethos of a strange country or culture I would soon be entering. Mary must have known that also.

It is uncertain what scripture texts were read at her funeral. However, in her 1992 University of Toronto Convocation address to the graduates, she quoted,

If you continue in my word, you are truly my disciples; and you will know the truth, and the truth will make you free. (John 8.31-32 NRSV)

She continued, "I believe in truth. It is the beginning of every thought. I take the quest for truth to mean to continue to educate yourselves, all your lives to be open to experience, to test things with an open mind and a keen expression, to have the courage to care deeply about such matters as social justice...life is an adventure. I can testify to that with every fibre of my 88 year-old self. The adventure has to do with love but also mostly with the search for truth. When you have truth you have meaning. When you have meaning you have it all."

I applaud her understanding of truth. She knew it is not a fixed entity, a fortress against all others, but an ongoing search and exploration. Ted Scott, Primate of the Anglican Church (see p. 120 of this book) once told me that when he had been a witness in court and asked to swear to tell "the truth, the whole truth, and nothing but the truth," he responded by saying that no one could know the whole truth. However he would swear to tell the truth that he knew, even if it were partial.

"When you have meaning, you have it all," she said. She struggled with what it meant to grow up, marry, and raise children in a family and society where roles were given and gendered. We live in a different time, but who of us does not search for meaning for our lives? Isn't that what is going on with those who may never darken a church door, but who celebrate "spirituality but not religion," adopt Buddhist practices of meditation, practice yoga, crowd the courses on Religion in our universities, and search relentlessly for authentic human community in a depersonalized world? How the current faith communities respond to that search is critical for our ongoing relevancy.

Another text singularly appropriate to her life occurs to me:

I offer you the choice of life or death, blessing or curse. Choose life and then you and your descendants will live; love the Lord your God, obey him and hold fast to him: that is life for you.   (Deuteronomy 30.19–20 NEB)

This text was Moses' teaching that despair, death, and brokenness were not to be viewed as the final reality. Hope was rather rooted in the character of God who was not a prisoner of circumstance, but offered renewal through life's choices. Looking after the strangers and showing mercy to the widow and the fatherless reflect a choice for life, not death. Moses' teaching was not a rigid, codified teaching, but one offering inner renewal if people would faithfully keep the commandments of love and justice. To hoard wealth, to ignore the foreigner or refugee, meant suffering and despair. Therefore, choose life.

Mary chose life. She obviously believed life to be a great adventure, and she lived hers with unique individuality, unwavering commitment to what she discerned as truth, and unstinting generosity of spirit and material goods, against all odds. What does it mean for you to "choose life"?

Anne Gertrude Mutch, Canada
25 December 1926 – 17 October 2000

Teacher in Montreal, St Catharines; Feminist; Student Christian Movement; Work Camps in Agriculture, ON and Industry, Quebec ('45–'46); School teacher in Toronto; Accompanied her husband Bruce to Japan to work for the Anglican Church of Canada with University students; gym teacher at YWCA in Nagoya, Japan; ('55) board member of Canadian Academy in Kobe, Japan; in Retirement Parish rep. on The Primate's World Relief and Development Fund; 10 Days for Global Justice; Save the Ajax Waterfront; Home for battered women. Died prematurely as a result of a traffic accident; Twin to Sandy, married to Bruce, one son and one daughter, grandchildren.

"I don't have any trouble with my wife," declared a Presbyterian delegate from Australia to the members of the World Council of Churches' Central Committee meeting in 1988. He was responding to the announcement by the Women's Unit of a program inviting Churches around the world to participate in the Ecumenical Decade for Churches in Solidarity with Women in Church and Society ('88–'98). Women around the world knew that although they constituted the great majority in their own congregation, they were usually denied participation in the decision-making apparatus of their denomination at that time. Also missing the point of the program, a Prelate from the UK then announced (presumably to the women at the meeting), "We'll give you a year." I exploded and said, "We are not asking you to give us anything. We are announcing a new program of the WCC. And judging by the comments I have heard, it will take at least ten years."[3] Three or four of us in the WCC had proposed the program, which, after much debate, was finally being formally launched by the WCC. As part of an ecumenical team visiting Panama churches to monitor the program, I later became aware that while it raised the consciousness of many men as well as women in the congregations, church leaders willingly entertained us royally for dinner, but were less willing to sit down and seriously look at the secondary position of women in the churches at that time. The Women's Unit of the WCC came to the same conclusion.

I worked with Anne Mutch on that program in Canada. She was a seasoned advocate for women in church and society. Bright and articulate, she was a teacher by profession. Being of the same generation, we had been involved in playing in church volleyball leagues and in summer camps sponsored by Canadian Girls in Training (CGIT) in Winnipeg in the 1940s. But I knew Anne best primarily through our mutual involvement with the Manitoba Student Christian Movement in university days. Here she learned her social and political advocacy, which she later married with her theology. One year she was Assistant to SCM Secretary Ted Scott, who later became Primate of the Anglican Church of Canada (see p. 120 of this book). Later, she and her Anglican priest husband Bruce worked for some years at the Nagoya Student Centre with university students in Japan, and for a number of social causes after retirement in Canada—all of them seeking to establish justice for people who had been marginalized or discarded by society.

Of the many scripture texts read at her funeral, I will concentrate on the following two:

> *Ho, everyone who thirsts, come to the waters; and you that have no money, come, buy and eat! Come buy wine and milk without money and without price. Why do you spend your money for what is not bread, And your labour for that which does not satisfy? Listen carefully to me and eat what is good, and delight yourselves in rich food. Incline your ear, and come to me; listen so that you may live. I will make with you an everlasting covenant, my steadfast, sure love for David. See, I made him a witness to the peoples, a leader and commander for the peoples. See, you shall call nations that you do not know, and nations that*

---

3 Many claim I said this publicly, and although I have no memory of it, it is certainly what I thought.

do not know you shall run to you, because of the Lord your God, the Holy One of Israel, for he has glorified you. (Isaiah 55.1–5 NRSV)

You shall indeed go out with joy and be led forth in peace.
(Isaiah 55.12 NEB)

What appropriate texts for Anne! She had caught a vision of the future through the summer Agricultural and Industrial SCM Work Camps she attended. The SCM students lived together in community. They worked in a wide variety of industrial jobs, or in the fields. They pooled their pay cheques. They prayed and worshipped together. They shared their experiences, their despair, and their dreams. They tried to link their faith with that "other" community—that of factory workers, bridging the class divide that separated university students from labourers. They shared with them efforts for better working conditions and examined a possible Christian response

Anne was a labourer by day, sharing the labourer's repetitive, meaningless work, whether weeding sugar beet fields or screwing tops on bottles. She gradually realized that her life was inextricably tied to theirs. She was a student by evening, engaging with her SCM community in an analysis of the labour conditions, the economic and societal realities, and understanding her interdependence with her sister labourers. This disciplined community supported her hope for a better society. Her experience helped her establish her life priorities as engagement in society for those "in exile": those without hope or a future, whether it be factory workers, trapped middle-class housewives, agricultural labourers in the sugar beet fields, or, later, battered women, poverty stricken people of the global south, or the environment itself: the endangered Ajax waterfront. This vision of hope informed her life and work, both in Japan and then in her own Ajax neighbourhood.

There is urgency in the Biblical text, anticipating a joyous secure future for the returning exiles, if only they will listen! Instead of the blatant expensive consumerism of Babylon, they are offered free rich food and wine. If they choose their community identity and live it now, they will be truly free at last! To claim that identity and be supported by it will preclude any further slavery.

What does the passage signal to us? This text is even more urgent for us today, in a world full of so much cynicism, pessimism, or skepticism about the future. Many people live without hope, and in that sense are in exile. The current faith community in the West and North is declining in strength, numbers, and influence, and feeling more and more as "being in exile." Why give one's life over to the demands and rewards of the marketplace and the current rat race, which yields no lasting satisfaction, and postpones everything until retirement, the text asks? Why not give your best energies to life-giving activities? Do you not know who you are? Do you not remember the community to which you belong? Here is a clarion call to the faith community to reclaim its collective identity, supported by all people of faith who have gone before, and to embrace change, visions of the future, and building a new world. It urges us as a community to forsake the junk food and ideology of the consumer-driven, anxiety-producing exploitative Empire that surrounds us. In the Empire, torture with impunity, shredding of human rights, and environmental abuse and collapse have become the norm. Here is the invitation to feast on the "free water, free wine, and free milk"[4] that are readily available through entering the community that invites the practice of compassion, mercy, generosity, forgiveness, and justice. Easier said than done of course. To embrace countercultural values in a community that has left the mainstream, as the gospel enjoins us to do, is scary, especially when so many of us enjoy and profit from things as they are.

This text, which is ours as well as that of the Biblical exiles, promises an everlasting and unconditional covenant with the exiles, following on previous remembered covenants: Moses at Sinai and the Ten Commandments; Abraham and the land; Noah and the rainbow; Isaiah's vision of peace and hope for swords to become ploughshares and spears beaten into pruning hooks (Isaiah 2.4), but especially of the everlasting covenant made with David to reconstitute the monarchy (2 Samuel 7.11–16). Isaiah 55.12 highlights the procession of the faithful out of the captivity of Empire into a changed situation. They will build and plant as Jeremiah urged (Jeremiah 31.4–5), and become more reliant on their new community of faith rather than on the old systems of the Empire. The returning exiles have a story of a covenant of mercy and compassion to tell, which inspires hope. It is a different story from that told by those around them. For many of us, the Isaiah 55 text is our story also, and we continue to sing it ("You Shall Go Out with Joy," VU # 884).

---

4   Walter Brueggemann, *Isaiah 40–66* (Louisville, KY: Westminster John Knox Press, 1998), p. 159

William (Bill) Norrie, OC, Canada
21 January 1929 – 6 July 2011

Mayor of Winnipeg ('79), the first of five successful elections; Graduate ('50) and Board of Regents of United College (now University of Winnipeg); Rhodes scholar ('53); Lawyer ('54); Politician; Developed "The Forks," the revitalization of the Exchange and Chinatown; The River Work; Habitat for Humanity, Winnipeg Symphony; United Way; Chancellor of University of Manitoba ('01); Honorary Consul General of Japan ('01); Order of Manitoba ('00); Lifelong member United Church of Canada. Married to Helen, father of three, grandfather of three.

I first met Bill Norrie through my husband, Roy. From childhood they both belonged to St. Paul's United Church, Winnipeg. After Bill had married Helen they bought "Elephant Island" on Lake of the Woods. I once tented on "Wilson Point" on that same island, with my four children, when my husband Roy had been compelled to return to Winnipeg for some emergency during our holidays. So we knew each other well. Although Bill excelled at almost everything he did, he was never boastful or arrogant. He was a remarkable leader who understood leadership as servanthood in the city where he lived. Here is scripture so appropriately chosen for his funeral by his minister, Barbara Janes.

> *Yahweh Sabaoth says this. "I am coming back to Zion and shall dwell in the middle of Jerusalem. Jerusalem will be called Faithful City....Old men and old women will again sit down in the squares of Jerusalem; every one of them staff in hand because of their great age. And the squares of the city will be full of boys and girls playing in the squares...I will bring my people back to live inside Jerusalem. They shall be [my people] and I will be their God in faithfulness and integrity.... For I mean to spread peace everywhere; the vine will give its fruit, the earth its increase, and heaven its dew....I intend in the present day to confer benefits on Jerusalem....Do not be afraid. These are the things that you must do. Speak the truth to one another; let the judgments at your gates be such as conduce to peace; do not secretly plot evil against one another; do not love false oaths; since all this is what I hate. It is Yahweh who speaks."*
> (Zechariah 8.3-5, 8, 12, 15-17 Jerusalem Bible)

"On a bike ride in Winnipeg," Rev. Barb Janes said at his funeral, "I stopped to watch a powwow. For one dance all the spectators were invited to participate—so aboriginal folk in traditional regalia or shorts and T-shirts, German tourists, and some locals, including an Orthodox Jew and his family—all dancing together. It was a glimpse of the peaceable world that is possible, and it happened in a place that Bill Norrie made possible: "The Forks" (the intersection of the Red and Assiniboine Rivers, Winnipeg, Manitoba.). It is the place where historic meetings of First Nations took place. Here is a glimpse of the Faithful City spoken of in Zechariah—of the old visiting and sitting, and the boys and girls playing in the squares.

And what does this text signify for the faith community that nurtured Bill? The people of Israel, having been carried away into exile by Babylon, express their pain, rage, and grief at God's silence, in Psalm 137 (RSV): "By the waters of Babylon, there we sat down and wept, when we remembered Zion" (i.e., Home). Many older people today feel themselves to be "in exile" when they remember the church they used to know. Many of the older generation remember their church as the centre of the community. Now that is not the case. The hymns are different; there are fewer home pastoral visits; many congregations are devoid of people under sixty; social networking has replaced youth groups; fewer people attend church. For some it causes pain and a sense of exile from what was familiar and prized. "How shall we sing the Lord's song in a foreign land?" (Psalm 137.4 RSV)

Along with this major change with the church is the loss of a sense of "place" where people used to live. Now, for all their merits and assets, many of us live in somewhat dysfunctional cities where you lock your door, as crime abounds; drive your kids to school to outwit the predators; drive bumper to bumper even though that increases pollution; live in a neighborhood or a condo where knowing another's name may be purely coincidental; and live in a world of failed states where people want to kill each other, and where the rich get richer and the poor, poorer.

We know we can't go back. Now, Canada is a country which previous generations never imagined: a mosaic of peoples made rich with their various cultures and gifts. Now, we live in a global village, which holds great promise as well as threat to our lives. We can be in instant touch with someone half way around the world with the touch of a button. Now we do not want to go back to what was, even if it were possible. Yet through all the change we long for a sense of "home;" for a vibrant community that supports us; for personal friendships that nurture us; for a roof over our head and food to eat; for refuge from the storms; and for acceptance without judgment.

When will there be a homecoming? Can we imagine one? Zechariah's poetry envisions a future for the return of the exiles from a grieving, scattered, despairing community in Babylon who cannot imagine new beginnings, to restored relationships in Jerusalem. He envisions a peaceable and well-ordered city where Israel can unlearn the ways of war, embrace the ways of international peace, and demonstrate joyous community.

Although it looks to those in exile that there is not much of a future, Zechariah tells us that God is able to bring about new beginnings—a new covenant. "They shall be my people and I will be their God, in truth and justice… do not be afraid…these are the things that you must do." And there follow some demands, which we would do well to re-read! It is when the exiles return, come home, renew their covenant, and practice truth and justice, that God's presence will become clear. The solo at Bill's funeral sounded the homecoming theme, as "Goin' Home" by Anton Dvorak was sung. Jeremiah buys a plot of land in Jerusalem, not as a real-estate investment, but as a token to symbolically signal hope for a future to the exiles as they prepare to return home.

Just as Bill loved his city and its people, so we are called to embrace the diversity of people and the needs of the cities where we live. Now most Canadians live in an urban culture; whether in rural areas or in cities. In what ways can we address the frightening anonymity of dwellers in an urban culture: the invisible barriers that exist between newcomers and established Canadians; the increasing city presence of First Nations dwellers; the needs of desperate refugees; the apathy of voters who consider all politicians crooks; the transportation gridlock; the reshaping of the very skyline of some few cities with the excessive number of high rises reaching to be the "highest"; the mounting heaps of garbage and disposal items of an affluent society; the unwillingness of many to accept higher taxes for increased services; the changes in communication technology?

This graffiti is painted on a wall on Christie St. near Davenport, where I live in Toronto: "Cities have the capacity of providing something for everybody, only because, and only when they are created by everyone" (Jane Jacobs). Is there a clue here to an authentic "homecoming?" If so, how is "everyone" to be motivated to participation?

Do faith communities have the spiritual energy to participate? Urban churches close and amalgamate at a frightening rate, yielding space to condos or trendy restaurants. If this continues, the "homecoming" will be replaced by a self-imposed exile of our faith community, as it flees the cities. If we continue to focus on the survival of an institution, rather than the needs of people outside the doors of the church, we will experience the failure of Zechariah's vision.

Our churches are called to embrace new patterns of being in city venues. Last year the Catholic Sisters of St. Joseph invited me to "Theology on Tap," a Monday night gathering at a nearby pub, which is the usual gathering place of some young adults who felt perfectly at home. I did not. The young people bought their own drinks; the pub owner gave the premises free as Monday was a slow night. The sisters provided the munchies and I provided the gospel imperative. The place was packed, the exchanges with me and with each other lively, and we concluded the evening with a prayer offered by a student. "We knew they were not going to come to us, so we went to them," said the Sisters. It will take imagination, trust, and the capacity to learn from ecumenical partners and from young adults themselves, to address and embrace the or needs of emerging generations of "unchurched" people who may not know the Lord's Prayer. Who knows whether any action on pubic policy in the city will emerge from such a gathering? But seeds are being sown.

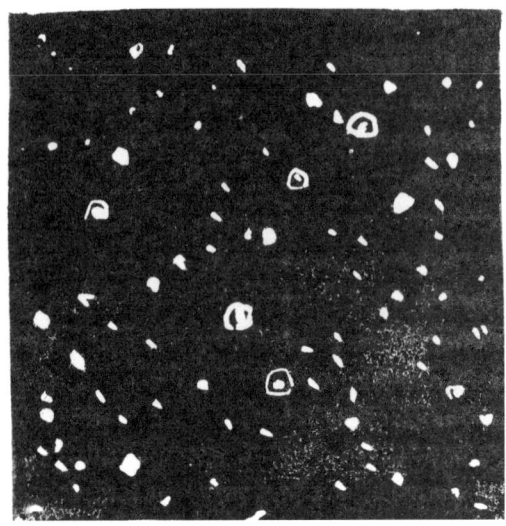

Edward (Ted) W. Scott, Canada

30 April 1919 – 21 June 2004

Primate of the Anglican Church of Canada ('71–'86); Ecumenist; Ordained an Anglican priest ('43); Social activist; Part-time Secretary of Vancouver Student Christian Movement ('45) and full time Secretary of Manitoba SCM ('45–49); Served Winnipeg parishes; Assoc. General Sec. of the Council for Social Service of the Canadian Church ('64); Bishop of Kootenay ('66–'71); Moderator of Central Committee of World Council of Churches ('75–'83); Member of Commonwealth "Eminent Persons Group" recommending implementation of sanctions against South Africa (late 80s); UN Canada Pearson Peace Prize ('88); Companion of the Order of Canada.

When he shall die / Take him and cut him out in little stars, / And he will make the face of heav'n so fine / That all the world will be in love with Night.[5]

The first thing Ted Scott did in 1945 when he came to Winnipeg to be the Secretary of the Manitoba Student Christian Movement was to involve us, the students, in opposing the internment of Japanese Canadians in the interior of the country. Canada was at war and the Canadian government viewed them as potential spies or traitors. For many of us, it was the beginning of a lifelong

---

5 William Shakespeare, *Romeo and Juliet* (3.2.21–24).

understanding of the gospel as social justice, and as having to do primarily with just relationships between people. I happened to be the SCM President for three years, and therefore thrust into a creative relationship with Ted at a formative time in my life. He became a theological mentor and a friend for the rest of his life.

Ted's primary commitment was always to the immediate needs of people. One evening when he was supposed to be showing the Manitoba SCM a film followed by discussion of some burning social issue, he had discovered a neighbour who had to harvest his potatoes that night before the frost came. We learned later that Ted had been delayed because he stopped to dig potatoes for his friend!

Ted had close ties with me as well as with some members of my immediate family over a number of years, and was important to my Christian formation. Here are a few instances. When he was SCM Secretary in Winnipeg in the 1940s, he came to know my father who at that time was Dean of Theology at United College (now the University of Winnipeg.) I sat in on many an informal theological conversation, and on occasion attended Anglican Church services. Ted was the only one who ever brought the Anglican liturgy alive for me, a gift for which I was eternally grateful. It was especially important later, when I ended up leading that same liturgy in Hamilton at First United/St. Thomas Anglican joint services in the 1970s after First United burnt to the ground and we moved across the street to be with the Anglicans. When he left the Winnipeg SCM in 1949, Ted recruited my husband Roy to succeed him. In the 1960s Ted met my sister Marjorie (see p. 58 of this book) in the Kootenays, BC. He had always been a supporter of the ecumenical movement, and during those years as Bishop of the Kootenays, he worked to establish shared congregations of Anglicans and United Church folk. My sister Marjorie was part of that.

Then came the icing on the cake. My term as Moderator overlapped with his as Primate, and we frequently enjoyed each other's company as well as similar theological postures when we appeared on pubic platforms together, or on CBC's "Man Alive" TV show with Roy Bonisteel. In 1983, when he was the outgoing Moderator of the Central Committee of the World Council of Churches, I was elected the incoming President, so Canadian continuity was maintained! There was a huge outcry in 1978 when, with Scott as Moderator, the WCC approved a $100,000 grant to the Zimbabwean Patriotic Front, and later to the Dene nation of Canada. I experienced some of the backlash two years later when I was Moderator, and the CBC and others accused us of funding "terrorist organizations." Religion and politics should be separate, they thundered. However, Ted cemented his ties with South Africa by being appointed by Prime Minister Mulroney as the Canadian member of the Commonwealth Eminent Persons Group in 1985 to try to help resolve the apartheid crisis in South Africa.

In the 1980s he was also appointed to review the health services to aboriginal peoples in Sioux Lookout, Northern Ontario, and encountered my daughter Ruth who was a doctor at the hospital. I still have the Christmas card we received that year, saying, "Lois and Ruth: It has been good to have established closer contact again. You both mean much to me. Please pass on word to your family members from me." And he meant much to us.

At Ted's funeral in 2004, the Hon. Adrienne Clarkson, Governor General of Canada, sat in the front pew and Archbishop Desmond Tutu came to deliver the homily. The Hon. Joe Clark read the following passage of scripture,

> *With what shall I come before the Lord, and bow myself before God on high? Shall I come before him with burnt offerings, with calves a year old? Will the Lord be pleased with thousands of rams, with ten thousands of rivers of oil? Shall I give my firstborn for my transgression, the fruit of my body for the sin of my soul? He has told you, O mortal, what is good; and what does the Lord require of you but to do justice, and to love kindness, and to walk humbly with your God?*
>
> (Micah 6.6–8 NRSV)

Ted spoke out courageously on controversial justice issues such as abortion, ordination of women, the death penalty, apartheid, residential schools, and health care, to name a few. He advocated justice for same-sex relationships, and was highly visible riding on the Anglican "float" in the Toronto Gay Parade. He spoke out of his faith convictions, which sometimes annoyed conservative Anglicans but gave heart to his ecumenical friends. He was self-critical of the church as institution, yet loyal to the people who gathered week by week for worship.

Through all the battles he remained kind to his opponents, while attacking their position. He was soft-spoken, but firm and unyielding in his policies on justice. Through it all he always walked humbly. He had not a spark of unwarranted pride because of the high positions he held. I remember discussing with him the theft of my Order of Canada medal. "Oh," he said, "I keep mine in my bottom drawer. I'm glad of the Order for the sake of Canada, but I set no store by it." On one occasion we were both attending an ecumenical celebration of the Ethiopian Orthodox Church in Toronto, and all the religious dignitaries of various denominations were gathered in the vestry, preparing to enter the sanctuary. When Ted arrived, they were all showing and admiring their respective gorgeous Bishops' rings. When someone asked Ted what stone was encased in his Episcopal ring, he turned the remark away, kindly, but firmly. He put no store in that kind of frippery.

"Justice," said Ted, "is not bland reality, but enables people to give expression of the gifts they have received from God the Creator. The church must learn to serve the poor, the helpless, the distraught, without dominating them. We must serve in a way that sets people free to serve, that doesn't build dependencies."[6]

What does this Micah text mean for the church of today and tomorrow? One of the hallmarks of the United Church of Canada has been its unwavering commitment to social justice over the years. I hope we continue to do it ecumenically, even if it takes more time and trouble. We have tried to do it in such a way that dependencies are discouraged. But a few years ago, a team of Christians from the global south reported to us, after visiting churches across Canada, that most Canadian Christians mistake charity for justice; mistake a stimulating friendship for reconciliation; and mistake feeling sorry for repentance. Restoring these strong theological categories to the lives of ordinary Christians, they told us, should be the task of the churches here for the next generation.

I worry sometimes too that we forget the part about "walking humbly with our God" as Ted did. We are perceived by some as an all-out horizontal social justice movement, with no vertical God-ward dimension at all. I worry as to whether we know how to pray. Many ministers print all the prayers for a service, but if you are blind, or illiterate, or don't read English, you might as well stay home. Frequently those reading the prayers read them as though reading the minutes of a meeting, or address the congregation as though it were a sermon, and not a prayer to the Creator. I know spontaneous prayer has its dangers as well, but we seem to have lost any capacity to pray without a printed, prepared text. Surely well prepared prayers, whether offered orally or printed, should be offered with passion. Like making love.

What seeds is your congregation sewing to plant a new believing community outside the bounds of your own congregation?

---

6   Hugh McCullum, *Radical Compassion* (Toronto: ABC Publishing, 2003), p. 475.

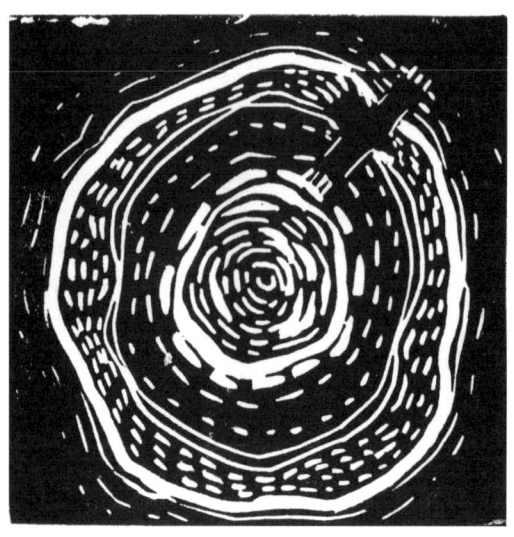

Mary Lynn (Mooney) Siwallace, Canadian

3 September 1946 – 6 November 2007

Ordained Minister of the United Church of Canada ('05); Nurse at Bella Coola Hospital; Home Care Nurse for her community of Nuxhalk First Nations, BC; Gained her M.Div. degree through the Native Ministry Education Program, Vancouver; Participant in Field trip of theological students to Guatemala; Served pastorate in Revelstoke, BC; Member of Healing Touch Canada, which she started when "deeply depressed"; Enjoyed clowning; Died at home in Bella Coola, BC. Married to Bruce, two sons, one grandson, extended family of "sons and daughters."

"The whites thought I was kind of not part of them anymore after my marriage to an aboriginal man," Mary Lynn told me. She was living in Bella Coola at the time, and working as a nurse in the United Church hospital. She totally distinguished herself in my eyes when I heard that when an aboriginal woman had run out of milk to nurse her baby, Mary Lynn (who was lactating at the time) immediately stepped in and completed the nursing.

I had met Mary Lynn in 1960 when Roy assumed the pastorate of First United Church in Thunder Bay. I was not yet ordained, but contracted part time as Community Minister, and as such responsible for Christian Education in the congregation as well. The United Church residential camp was nearby, but more mature girls had "done that." So we made a base camp on Lake Shebandowan and Mary Lynn, at age fifteen, joined in the day trips to various parts of the lake. It occurred to me that women might like to share the joys of canoe tripping through Quetico Provincial Park, with its magnificent network of waterways plied by the voyageurs many years earlier. It lay two hours west, and offered a perfect opportunity to canoe "the border lakes." I then offered a seven-day canoe trip to girls who were either in Grade 10 or fifteen years of age, and therefore strong enough to portage a canoe. They could also expect an hour of Bible study every day, and a worship service. Mary Lynn came along. She loved the warm rain experienced as we slogged through the mud on a rainy day portage near Pickerel Lake. She particularly loved dribbling cold water on those who did not respond with alacrity to a glorious new day.

I kept in touch with her as her faith matured and she subsequently decided to seek ordination in the United Church. As part of her theological training, she told me about a field trip to Guatemala where she spoke to survivors of the massacre that had occurred during the civil war when the country was under a brutal dictatorship. "The experience confirmed my faith so I can finally name where I'm at, at this point in time. God was with those mothers in their suffering,"[7] she said. Shortly after, she was ordained a Minister of the United Church of Canada.

"I experienced Healing Touch when I was deeply depressed," she told me. "With the touch of hands-on energy work, I had a vision of the tree of Life and a white eagle circling above me. People around me noticed the change....I learned to use Healing Touch, which is the heart of Jesus. It energizes people. It is a certain hands-on technique that connects and helps people who need spiritual guidance and prayers....It started with a group of nurses in the States. The healing pathway at Naramata Centre, BC, where I learned it, is basically the same but with a Christian aspect."[8]

She was sustained through a lengthy terminal illness by the musical refrain adaptation of Psalm 91 set to music,

---

7   Lois M Wilson, *Streams of Faith* (Toronto: United Church Publishing House, 2006), p. 140.
8   Lois M Wilson, *Streams of Faith*, p. 91.

> *And I will raise you up on eagle's wings,*
> *bear you on the breath of dawn,*
> *make you to shine like the sun,*
> *and hold you in the palm of my hand.* (VU p. 807)

She had the United Church's New Creed (VU, p. 918) recited as part of her funeral service, and had this verse from that musical adaptation of Psalm 91 engraved on her headstone: "I will raise you up on eagle's wings." She affirmed," The Spirit was so evident in the circling overhead of the eagles who were always a sign of God's presence for me." The strength and spiritual power of this psalm that energized Mary Lynn in her dying runs parallel to the following passage:

> *Have you not known? Have you not heard? The Lord is the everlasting God, the Creator of the ends of the earth. He does not faint or grow weary; his understanding is unsearchable. He gives power to the faint, and strengthens the powerless. Even youths will faint and be weary, and the young will fall exhausted; but those who wait for the Lord shall renew their strength, they shall mount up with wings like eagles, they shall run and not be weary, they shall walk and not faint.*
> (Isaiah 40.28–31 NRSV)

The New English Bible has this translation, "they will grow wings like eagles" (Isaiah 40.31). I like that translation. Through a telescope I once watched eagles ascending and soaring over the Rockies. They just went up, and up, and up and finally over. What a fantastic experience if I too could soar like that!

Here is poetry and vision that addresses our spiritual fatigue and apathy, resulting from our indecision about making a faith commitment, or because we have settled in and accepted the way things are. We have given up believing and working for social justice, or family harmony, or opposing the arms race, or the redemption of the environment. It is too tiring and with few positive results. There are not enough people involved. We are "weary, faint, and exhausted."[9] This is what I sense people mean by "burn-out." Of course if you depend entirely on your own resources you will soon experience burn out. This text reminds us that newness and hope are not ours to create. They are a gift, and this text points to the Creator as the source of all spiritual energy and newness. When it happens, it

---

9 Walter Brueggemann, *Isaiah 40–66*, p. 27

astounds us. And we are delivered from the pride of assuming everything depends on our efforts, or inversely of settling for the status quo. There is a warning here. It all depends on "waiting," that social activists like me find hard to do. But it is reminiscent of the Biblical phrase, "In the fullness of time." If one's life posture is predicated on trust that the Creator of all that is, in fact, is biased toward justice and equity and compassion, then "waiting" for the definitive action from that same Creator makes eminent sense. The source of energy for the running and the walking, for the "new thing," will manifest itself in due time.

How do you renew your spiritual energy? What practices or discipline do you follow? Have you shared this with other people? What have you learned from other people?

Rhea Menzel Whitehead, Canadian, born in USA

22 January 1936 – 14 June 2011

Ecumenist; Feminist; Facilitator of just global relationships; Missiologist; educator; Lay theologian; Studied Cantonese at Yale University; Moved to Hong Kong ('61); To Toronto to work with Joint Centre On Modern East Asia, University of Toronto and York University ('76); Later Asia Area Administrator for both Anglican and United Churches of Canada; General Sec. of the Division of World Outreach of the United Church of Canada ('92); In retirement, taught at Silliman University, Philippines, and Nanjing Union Theological Seminary, China. Key role in talks between North and South Korea; Invited by Kim Dae-Jung of Korea to his Presidential inauguration; Hon. Doctorate from Emmanuel College. Married to Ray, three children, three grandchildren.

One Christmas, I was at a gathering where we were all asked to name our favourite Christmas hymn or carol. While many of us chose carols having to do with snow, fireplaces and good cheer, Rhea chose "When I Needed a Neighbour," (VU #600), which speaks of those hungry and thirsty, cold and naked, sick and wretched, needing healing. "And the creed and the colour and the name won't matter, were you there?" To her, this was the meaning of Christmas. Her faith was rooted in a sensitive awareness of the deprivations so many people experience daily.

I first met Rhea at the offices of the Canadian Council of Churches, Toronto, in 1979 when she was organizing a trip to visit China, which until then had been off Westerners' maps. Subsequently our paths crossed many times. One of my main memories is our week together in Tozanso, the International Youth Centre, in Japan soaking ourselves in the communal hot baths that guarantee complete relaxation. It was at that 1984 World Council of Churches consultation on "Peace and Justice in Northeast Asia" that official Christian delegations from North and South Koreans were brought together for the first time since World War II. Let me quote from an email sent to me from Eric Weingartner, the organizer of that meeting: "The stakes were enormous. One wrong move, one wrong decision, one wrong attitude could slam the door shut again for years to come....I knew I could depend on Rhea to give this fragile infant of reconciliation a fighting chance at life. Rhea had history in Asia and in Korea. She knew what the culture required...I am convinced that she can take at least a small amount of credit for what would later become the Sunshine policy of former President Kim Dae-Jung." That Tozanso meeting became a symbol of openness and hope.

Responsible for directing all the overseas work of the United Church in the 1990s, she was heavily involved in the Philippines when the church supported the National Democratic Front that was working for social justice opposing the brutal Marcos regime ('72–'86). On one occasion, temporary peace zones had been agreed upon and skirmishes abandoned. She and colleague Oh Jae Shik decided to visit a village, and made their way in a small Toyota over bumpy roads until they found themselves on top of a mountain with a beautiful panorama before them. Lovely terraced paddy rice fields were in evidence. "I enjoyed the view with Rhea. We had worked together for fifteen years so I put my arm around her and asked, 'How can God allow the destruction of such beauty?' wrote Jae Shik in an email to me. She sighed, squeezed my hand and replied, 'Jesus too had such moments but he refused mountain top experiences,' referring to the Transfiguration. Then she said with a determined voice that was all too familiar, 'Let's go down.'"

This is what that same Korean Oh Jae Shik wrote me when he received word of Rhea's impending death. "Many Asian countries turned to authoritarian rule and people aspiring for justice and democracy were cornered. We were pushed out to a waste land without being prepared to protect ourselves, as well as our organizations. Then came friendship and solidarity from all over the world. Rhea crossed walls, borders, obstacles endlessly for over half a century.

Now Rhea is headed for a borderless space..."

Rhea chose this text to be read at her funeral:

> *My joy is gone, grief is upon me, my heart is sick.... "The harvest is past, the summer is ended, and we are not saved." For the hurt of my poor people I am hurt, I mourn, and dismay has taken hold of me. Is there no balm in Gilead? Is there no physician there? Why then has the health of my poor people not been restored?*
>
> (Jeremiah 8.18, 20–22 NRSV)

"In 2001 while living in the Philippines, Rhea was invited to lead reflections at the triennial convocation of the National Council of Churches in the Philippines. She used this passage and song ("There Is a Balm in Gilead," VU #612) to reflect on the longing of people for justice and social health. Jeremiah asks despairingly if there is any balm, any hope for health for the hurting of his people. African-American slaves turned the words into affirmation and hope; *there is* a balm in Gilead. Rhea reflected at that time that "sin-sick" souls include those who have been sinned-against, who continue the struggle, who in spite of discouragement hang in and are revived by the spirit. In her last days Rhea particularly asked that this song be included when we remembered her and hoped that Mary Lou Fallis would perform it."[10] And that song was indeed sung at Rhea's funeral.

Rhea was deeply disturbed at a 1983 consultation in Burma when she discovered that all the delegates were male! Subsequently, she donated a special section of books on feminist theology to the Nanjing Theological Seminary Library in China. To be an advocate of feminist theology in a deeply Confucian culture with its rigidly defined social and gender roles could not have been easy. But she persisted, making sure scholarships were available for women studying theology in all parts of the world where the United Church had partners: Africa, Asia, Latin America, and India and wherever else she could exert influence.

She critiqued the practice of mission that was still tied to colonialism or domination. Instead, she paid attention to intercultural issues, and opted for companionship and partnership in such programs as Partnership Africa. She was a bridge builder between North America and the rest of the world.

At her funeral I offered this adaptation and reflection based on Hebrews 11.32–39 (NRSV) as appropriate for Rhea's work and witness:

---

10 Paul Menzel , "Why Rhea Chose this Passage," Printed in her Funeral bulletin, 2011.

> *And what more should I say? For time would fail me to tell of the faithful work of Rhea, who through faith established social justice; stood in solidarity with the oppressed; confounded the opposition; quenched the rhetoric of the Marcos regime; witnessed to promises of resurrection and new life of faithful souls; won strength through weakness; supported theological education for those undergirding the vision of a new heaven and earth; bonded with other women; visited the prisoner. Some were tortured; others raped; others suffered mocking, scourging and even chains in imprisonment. They were afflicted and ill-treated—of whom the world was not worthy. They are a great cloud of witnesses cheering us on. They are the communion of saints, among whom is Rhea Whitehead. They did not enter their promised inheritance, because, with us in mind, God had made a better plan, that they would not, apart from us, be made perfect.*

There's a stinger! "They would not, apart from us, be made perfect." In other words, whether they are judged faithful will depend on you and on me. The Apostles' Creed calls it "the communion of saints." To be in communion with them is not hoping for some word beyond the grave from Rhea. It is to be in solidarity with her and her work and to gain motivation and power for our work from her witness. We are bound together in the Christian fellowship.

How we can be involved in their struggle and witness for justice is a question for each of us to answer. Are we advocates for women in the global south, as well as women at the bottom of the heap in Canada? Or perhaps we visit prisoners? Or we struggle with how the United church can affirm in it liturgies with the nuances and understandings of cultures other than ours? Or we partner with people with disabilities far beyond building a ramp for their wheelchairs? Or our prayers regularly include victims of abuse or torture or suffering people we know or do not know? None of us can identify the particular faithfulness appropriate for anyone else. But Hebrews 12 points the direction for us.

It advises, "stiffen your drooping arms and shaking knees, and keep your steps from wavering" (Hebrews 12.12-13 NEB). So get cracking. Train yourself in Christian discipline. Pursue peace. Be open to grace for everyone. Do not let bitterness rule your life. Our destiny and our legacy are bound up with those who have gone before us, like Rhea. Did her faithfulness mean anything? Did it mean enough for us to follow her lead and extend her work? Think about it. Then do it.

Roy F. Wilson, Canada
9 April 1925 – 26 December 2005

My husband, ordained minister United Church of Canada ('49); Ecumenist; Secretary of Student Christian Movement, Manitoba ('50–'54); For over 40 years served pastorates in Canada: in Lyleton, MB; Atlantic Avenue United, Wpg; First Church United, Fort William (now Thunder Bay); First United Church, Hamilton; Chalmers United Church, Kingston; Timothy Eaton Memorial Church and Forest Hill United, Toronto; Represented UCC on World Methodist Council and World Alliance of Reformed Churches; Co-Chair of Constitutional Committee on Church Union ('70s); Co-Chair of International Theological Commission of the Anglican Consultative Committee; Chair of UCC Inter-Church, Inter-Faith Committee; Executive member of UCC General Council over several years; Member Judicial and Vacancies Committees. Married to Lois, four children, 12 grandchildren, one great-grandchild.

"I called Dad to say that I was pregnant with number five," our daughter Ruth told me. "I wish you would tell us something new sometimes," he responded. When asked if he had some particular Biblical text in mind for the preacher's use at his funeral, he responded wryly to the minister, "Surprise me."

I met my future husband at United College (now University of Winnipeg) when I was in Grade 12, through the SCM. I respected Roy Wilson for his obvious integrity, and enjoyed his sense of humour. He didn't talk a lot, but when he did, he would drop some memorable or witty phrase into the conversation. We had sometimes gone to dances together over the years, but more for convenience than for romance. Near the end of our theological training (I was one year behind him), we began to regard each other with more than friendly interest. Subsequently we were married—for 55 years, even though he had to polish the silver and pick the lilacs for our wedding in 1950.

On a trip to New Zealand, we stopped to explore a Maori church that boasted of its stained glass window of Jesus. It was positioned in such a way that when viewed from a certain angle, Jesus appeared to be actually walking on the water of the lake that was just beside the church. However there were signs warning against taking photos. I wanted to explore this further, so asked Roy if he would mind standing guard while I went into the church. When I came out, he told me he had finally found what he wanted to be engraved on his gravestone. He pointed to a nearby engraving, "He waited patiently."

He was endlessly patient. For the first 13 years of our marriage we took our family of four camping on Lake of the Woods. I was quite at home, but it was all new to him. Finally, he declared that he was opposed to spending our precious holiday time stuck in a tent on a rainy day, on an island, with four rambunctious kids. After he had persuaded me of the strength of his position, we bought a summer "camp" at Birch Beach on the shores of Lake Superior, and it became our favourite and beloved summer retreat for the rest of our lives.

He was an ecumenist from his earliest days at University through the Student Christian Movement, and became its staff secretary in Manitoba following Ted Scott (see p. 120 of this book). He represented the United Church at global gatherings of both Methodists and Presbyterians. He was eternally grateful for the Latin American Methodists who, having come through Argentina's "dirty war" of the late 1970s, bore strong testimony to the profound suffering and courageous opposition to the military dictatorship in their country, thus nullifying the vacuous stories of suburban Oklahoma Methodists.

When the first Muslim refugees fleeing Idi Amin of Uganda arrived in Hamilton, Roy made sure accommodation for them was reserved in First Place, a multi-purpose high rise replacing First United Church which had burnt to the ground in 1969. After the 1973 Chilean coup had deposed Allende, several socialist/communist Chilean doctors, fleeing for their lives, arrived in Hamilton and to our house on Christmas day. Our ecumenism was tested when one of them saw our Christmas tree and dismissed it as a "bourgeois affectation."

We worked together in team ministry for 15 years in local congregations. He claimed that the preacher could be relevant to the congregation only in so far as he had pastored them and shared their griefs and celebrations, and was happy that the role of preacher and pastor was combined in most of his pastorates. Roy was stable, well grounded, and knew who he was. He was an anchor for me, and that undergirded our relationship when, as he would often comment drily, "Lois was flitting off somewhere to save the world." Stan Lucyk, who conducted Roy's funeral, pointed out that the words describing him—solid, grounded, stable—were all rooted in the Hebrew Biblical word for "faith." It is the word *aymun,* from which we derive "Amen." The word "faith" implies a relationship, a holding firm, a saying "Amen" to God. It was our daughter Jean who saw the extension of this quality when she identified the words from John's letter that went into Roy's relationship with his children and grandchildren. "We love because he first loved us" (1 John 4.19 NRSV).

He died very suddenly at home when his heart gave out. Later, what ran through my head when I replayed that last moment as I supported him with my arms was that line from *King Lear,* "Why should a dog, a horse, a rat, have life, / And thou not breath at all?"[11]

Roy had thought deeply about his funeral. He had attended a funeral where some six speakers had eulogized the deceased, and he complained, "God scarcely got a mention." So he insisted "it was not to be a service to celebrate Roy, but rather the Creator who led him wondrously through this life." He didn't want eulogy. He wanted gospel. He chose Psalm 23.

> *The Lord is my shepherd, I shall not want. He makes me lie down in green pastures; he leads me beside still waters; he restores my soul. He leads me in right paths for his name's sake. Even though I walk through the darkest valley, I fear no evil; for you are with me; your rod and your staff—they comfort me. You prepare a table before me in the presence of my enemies; you anoint my head with oil; my cup overflows. Surely goodness and mercy shall follow me all the days of my life, and I shall dwell in the house of the Lord my whole life long.*
>
> (Psalm 23 NRSV)

At the funeral, Stan Lucyk's sermon concentrated on the image of the Bedouin

---

11 William Shakespeare, *King Lear,* (5.3.304–05).

host rather than the image of shepherd. Moffatt's Bible translation accurately translates verse 5 as "You are my host, spreading a feast before me, while my foes have to look on. You pour oil upon my head, my cup is brimming over." The passage highlights two laws of the desert—that of revenge and that of hospitality.

The law of revenge came from the responsibility of the tribe to protect its weak members, Stan explained. Someone was therefore appointed to avenge the blood of a kinsman by the death of the one who shed it. Is the psalmist depicting something he had seen in the desert—a fugitive from blood vengeance fleeing across the desert with avengers on his trail? Ahead of the fugitive lies a Bedouin's tent and he knows therein lies safety. In that tent, Bedouin hospitality overrules vengeance. The host will anoint his guest's head with oil, set out the best food he has, and fill the guest's cup to overflowing. Outside the tent, the avengers look on helplessly. "You prepare a table before me in the presence of my enemies." The law of hospitality trumps the law of vengeance. But only for a limited time. For only two days and the intervening night he is safe.

"Surely goodness and mercy shall follow me" (Psalm 23.6 NRSV) is better translated, "goodness and kindness pursue me, every day of my life" (Psalm 23.6 Jerusalem Bible). God's mercies go on and on. We will be welcome in "the house of the Lord for ever" (Psalm 23.6 RSV) We have guest privileges without time limit. "For ever." Not even death stops God's hosting, because God is that kind of host. Surely the One who worked the miracle of Creation will work the miracle of new life, of resurrection.

The image of the hospitable table invites us to generosity, not greed. God is always preparing tables of abundance for us, multiplying loaves and fish, cooking fish at the seashore, renewing the supply of wine, welcoming the widow, the orphan, the foreigner. Again there is sounded that unbelievable conviction in God's unfailing generosity. Roy reflected that generosity in his own life.

Do we really believe we have guest privileges forever? How can this be, and how is it made manifest? What is our part in it?

CHAPTER 4

The Church and the World

John Beaton Laughton Carrel, QC, Canada

23 December 1924 – 24 December 2000

Lawyer: Naval veteran; Founding partner in CARREL and partners law firm; Skier; Member and Clerk of Session of First Church United, Thunder Bay; Federally and politically a Conservative; Lawyer for inaugural Thunder Bay Community Foundation. Married to Ada, three children, two grandchildren, numerous nieces and nephews.

"Come in your skiing clothes," the poster said. Many did. It was their invitation to a special 9.00 a.m. Sunday service of worship at First Church United, Thunder Bay, set early to accommodate skiers who could be on the ski hills well before noon. John Carrel, the Clerk of Session, conceived this workable idea in a city that boasted accessible skiing, and whose working people (many of whom were church members) counted on weekends for skiing. This was not an attempt to put sports before church. This was an attempt to accommodate faithful church-goers who happened also to be avid skiers and whose main free time for skiing fell on a Sunday. I fully supported the early service, since I too am a skier.

I met and worked with John in Thunder Bay, Ontario, between 1960 and 1969 when Roy and I were ministers at First Church United. He often urged me to be ordained, pointing out that I was already doing the work of an ordained minister. "Might as well formalize it with ordination," he said. On the initiative and with the backing of the congregation, it finally happened, even though I was unable (and unwilling) to accept settlement elsewhere as we had four children under twelve at the time.

For whatever reasons, Presbytery allowed me to be settled as the second minister, in team with my husband Roy, at First Church. We were one of the first "team ministries" in the United Church. I have often said that he did the "in-house" work (most of the preaching and pastoral care) and I did the "out-house" work (Christian education of adults and youth and their witness in the community). We took turns administering baptism after one mother refused to have her baby baptized by me, a female minister. Another congregant wanted to know if I knew how to conduct a funeral. Perhaps it was because such a thing had never been seen in those days, and it was beyond imagination that it could ever happen. These were, after all, the very early days of ordained women in the United Church of Canada.

When I was appointed to the Senate, John wrote me, "Generally, based on those I have known personally, I have great respect for those who serve in the Parliament and the Legislature. As in all cases, there are exceptions, and on the political side, the exceptions are all we hear about. Of course we did get the odd brief accolade for the likes of Tommy Douglas. A word from Gandhi might be appropriate, 'I can say without the slightest hesitation, and yet in all humility, that those who say religion has nothing to do with politics do not know what religion means.'" It was widely known that Tommy Douglas was a preacher, and accolades for his work as a Parliamentarian in the secular news always mentioned that fact. John was one of the strongest supporters of the church's involvement in "Town Talk," a city wide program described elsewhere in this book (see pp. 17–19), inviting citizens to identify and work together on issues important to their collective future.

In his own obituary (which he wrote because his cancer afforded him some time), he confessed obliquely, publicly, and for the first time, "Along the way he learned that alcoholism sharpens the sensitivity of men's souls." He chose 1 Corinthians 13.4–8 and 2 Timothy 4.6–8 for his funeral, as well as this passage, appropriate for a man who was both a political and religious leader in his community, but also had grave and serious personal weaknesses which were widely known:

> *...on my own behalf I will not boast, except of my weaknesses. But if I wish to boast, I will not be a fool, for I will be speaking the truth....Therefore, to keep me from being too elated, a thorn was given me in the flesh, a messenger of Satan to torment me, to keep me from being too elated. Three times I appealed to the Lord about this, that is would leave me, but he said to me, "My grace is sufficient for you, for power is made perfect in weakness." So, I will boast all the more gladly of my weaknesses, so that the power of Christ may dwell in me. Therefore I am content with weaknesses, insults, hardships, persecutions, and calamities for the sake of Christ; for whenever I am weak, then I am strong.*
>
> (2 Corinthians 12.5-6a, 7b-10 NRSV)

John chose this text himself, believing it totally appropriate for his own life. He was well aware of his human failings, struggling mightily with his weaknesses, and depended upon the grace of God and the fellowship of the congregation to support him. He continued to be a leader as Clerk of Session despite his human frailties, knowing that the essence of Christian life is not "setting a good example" (he would have failed that one!) but being open to the surprising grace and forgiveness of God. Was it because he knew his weaknesses that he was able to empathize so closely with the weaknesses of others? When he was Clerk of Session, John and my husband discovered that the person trusted with counting and banking the weekly congregational offerings had been skimming off a substantial amount of money for the needs of her large family. It was fraud pure and simple. Rather than call in the police and rob the eight children of a mother for some time, they decided to deal with her weakness privately, justly, and compassionately. The person in question began to understand and face her own weakness, and in that lay her emerging strength.

Isn't that the scandal of Christianity? That weakness is strength? That vulnerability can be redemptive? Why is it then that the church keeps trying for numbers, success, entitlement, influence, which are not even gospel categories? Almost everything I have learned about strength and redemption has been from those on the edge of society–the South African blacks in apartheid days confined to reservations who nevertheless engaged in a long standing freedom struggle and prevailed; the Micmac women of New Brunswick who, stripped of treaty rights including medical care and property should they marry a white man, kept on until that was reversed. I learned as an honorary member of an Alcoholics Anonymous group about depending on a Greater Power and the fragility of that dependence. I learned with that group of the need to name the disease of alcoholism for what it is: to de-stigmatize alcoholic persons and to support rather than condemn them in their terrible weakness. Why is it we hesitate to believe that out of weakness comes strength? Should not the remnant of the church be waiting for, receiving, and witnessing to God's transforming grace and mercy, and then acting on it in situations such as these, rather than lamenting our loss of status and influence?

Here is a tale of two calendars. I came across a Salvation Army calendar that had photos of hungry, destitute people living in abandoned laneways amid desolate surroundings. It was a portrait of discomfort and ugliness. The United Church calendar had photos of handsome churches on the banks of beautiful streams, or interior views of polished pews and stained glass windows. It was a portrait of comfort and beauty. The difference was striking. One said to me, "I was hungry and you gave me food. I was thirsty and you gave me something to drink." It called the viewer into mission outside the sanctuary. The arrows pointed outward. The other said, "Look how beautiful our sanctuary is. Come inside and see it." The arrows pointed inward. I wondered where I would most fully experience the grace of God?

The way ahead for the United Church will not be the same way as we have known in the past. So many congregations are weakened because of loss of members. Might that weakness be strength? Might that weakness lead members to pay more attention to the mystery of God in their lives? Might that weakness signal to us a profound need to experience, share, and speak with others of the depth and wonder of the grace of God? Might that newly discovered strength also lead us to entertain with hope new and imaginative shapes of the church that we had never imagined possible? To marry our solidarity with the hungry and destitute with our knowledge of God as one of justice and compassion?

And what about new patterns of ministry? Might we look at the "worker priest" model developed in France some years ago? They were fully trained and ordained priests working part time in the congregation, but supporting themselves financially by retaining a secular job. That would balance congregational members who earn their living in secular jobs as well, and who exercise their congregational responsibilities part time. All would take seriously their call to the priesthood of all believers. Out of perceived weakness comes strength.

John Robert (Rob) Cotton, Canada

12 November 1913 – 9 July 2009

Carpenter; Gymnast (performed professionally on stage, ice and roller rink); Carpenter; Photographer; Former lab technician; Educated in Winnipeg; Worked at Canada Car and Abitibi Mission Mill in Thunder Bay after moving there ('41); trained the "Tumbling Dominoes," a troupe of 30 young people who performed out of the YMCA (the Cotton Family was also a popular acrobatic act); Elder and steward of United Church. Married to Betty; three children, many grandchildren.

He was a man of many parts. Trained as a lab technician, and working at the Manitoba Medical College in Winnipeg, he was also a first-class carpenter and gymnast, attending Central Methodist Church in that city. The Methodist abstinence from all alcohol never really "took" with Rob, and he enjoyed a drink with the best of them. Brought up and nurtured in that congregation, he treasured hymns and his beloved Psalm 23. Despite the fact that at age 19 he was distracted enough to call out "Betty" to the attractive animated 14-year-old at the Sunday school rally, he did pay some attention to his teachers.

There at the youth rallies, he began to show more than ordinary interest in Betty and predictably they married, and then in 1941 moved to what was then known as Fort William (now Thunder Bay, Ontario). Neither of them anticipated

CHAPTER 4 CHURCH AND THE WORLD ▪ 143

that their marriage would last 68 years. They settled on the banks of the Kam River, where Rob exercised his carpentry skills and built their comfortable home that later housed them and their family of three children.

Rob and Betty were among the first people to welcome Roy and me into our pastorate at First Church United in 1960. They invited us to visit their home on one of the first nights after our arrival. It turned out the smelt were running, and it was our first introduction to that special event. Equipped with rubber boots and hand nets, we found it very exciting to fish these small things out of the river in the inky darkness, relieved only by the beam of a flashlight. I even came to love eating fried smelts.

Rob had a wonderful and unique sense of humour, was delightfully irreverent, and punctuated false piety, sentimental religiosity and religious posturing at every turn. He never tired of telling jokes about his roots in Summerside, PEI Both his humour and his faith gave him a perspective on life that allowed him to relax and not take himself too seriously, all of which made him a good friend of my husband Roy. The two would sometimes motor up the river and go fishing for the day.

He was a man of some physical strength and an accomplished gymnast par excellence. A talented hand balancer and "top man," he performed professionally on stage, ice and roller rink. A high ladder or scaffolding would invite a spontaneous handstand. His grandchildren knew him as "the grandpa who walks on his hands." Turning his skills to the Lakehead's eager youth, he formed and trained the "Tumbling Dominoes," a troupe of thirty young men and women who performed out of the YMCA. The Cotton family became a popular acrobatic act throughout the district. "Leave them laughing and wanting more," was his mantra. At the Cottons' 50th wedding anniversary celebration, their son Cuyler spoke of their acrobatic show, but also of their lives together. He told the guests, "my father always provided a safety net lest any of us were to fall during one of our acts—or in our lives." After age 88, when Rob climbed to the roof of his house to repair things, he had to do it when the neighbours weren't around, as they would have prevented him.

He knew the Christian narrative well, and tried to live out its essence. Scriptures read at his funeral were the well-known texts of Micah 6, Psalm 23, and Revelation 21, all of them affirming the moral significance of human actions. Since I have commented on these texts elsewhere, I have chosen to highlight a text that he taught his children.

> *All the nations will be gathered before him, and he will separate people one from another as a shepherd separates the sheep from the goats, and he will put the sheep at his right hand and the goats at the left. Then the king will say to those at his right hand, "Come, you that are blessed by my Father, inherit the kingdom prepared for you from the foundation of the world; for I was hungry and you gave me food, I was thirsty and you gave me something to drink, I was a stranger and you welcomed me, I was naked and you gave me clothing, I was sick and you took care of me, I was in prison and you visited me." Then the righteous will answer him, "Lord, when was it that we saw you hungry and gave you food, or thirsty and gave you something to drink? And when was it that we saw you a stranger and welcomed you, or naked and gave you clothing? And when was it that we saw you sick or in prison and visited you?" And the king will answer them, "Truly I tell you, just as you did it to one of the least of these who are members of my family, you did it to me."* (Matthew 25.32-40 NRSV)

Nurtured as a Methodist in Winnipeg, he knew that the proof of the pudding was in the eating. Knowing the days of the Depression in Canada, he resonated to the Matthew text. He knew that the essence of the spiritual life was not the singing of hymns but the practice of radical hospitality and the non-judgmental assistance to anyone in need. His home was a hospitable one, open particularly to First Nations people from the north. He demonstrated by his behaviour his most profound convictions about the meaning of our short lives.

He lived an exceptionally long life, and had to struggle with the slow decline of his faculties and loss of his remarkable physical abilities. Where was the meaning then? A man of impressive spirituality, when the end was near he took the hand of his wife Betty and said, "God has something to do with all this!" So he was a theologian to boot.

A man of many parts: carpenter, church elder and steward, accomplished gymnast, self-taught photographer, theologian, father, a "grandpa who walks on his hands" who practiced hospitality to strangers and to friends alike. "His life was gentle, and the elements / So mix'd in him that Nature might stand up / And say to all the world, 'This was a man!'"[1]

---

1 William Shakespeare, *Julius Caesar* (5.5.73-75).

Minnie Ada Freeman, Canada

10 August 1890 – 17 December 1969

My mother; Practiced generous hospitality through perpetual open house; Before marriage, taught Home Economics in Kincardine, Ottawa, Brandon and Olds School of Agriculture, Alberta; Creative and unique personality; Authored pageants; "Freeman slides" on the global work of the United Church of Canada; Budding artist; Enjoyed leatherwork, sewing and knitting. Married to my father, E.G.D. Freeman (Dean of Theology, United College); five children, 21 grandchildren.

I first met Mother when I was born in Winnipeg, on 8 April 1927, the last of five children. Stories about her abound. Recently I met Brock Saunders, who was ordained the same time as I was, and he said to me, "If anyone has ever met your mother, they will never forget her." A few years ago I was driving to Niagara on the Lake to meet my daughter Jean and granddaughter Lois for a play at the Shaw Festival. A few miles short of my destination, my car suddenly stalled, and everything went dead. I had no cell phone but was within a short walk of a Tim Horton's. I wondered how to let my daughter know of my delay, and how to get to Niagara on the Lake? When I was deliberating, I noticed someone come into Tim Horton's whom I recognized as Charles Catto, of Frontiers Foundation. "What are you doing here?" he asked of me. "I know what you are doing here,"

I responded. "I am stranded, and hopefully, you might drive me to Niagara on the Lake." "I will," he said," because of what your mother once did for me. I had just come down to Winnipeg from northern Manitoba for a few days of rest. Of course I stayed with your folks—everybody did. When she found out I was staying over the Sunday, she phoned the minister of the biggest congregation in town and got him to ask me to preach about my work as a United Church missionary up in God's lake in northern Manitoba. So I did, and I owe her one."

Mother tailored the world to her own needs. Because she was short, she cut down the legs of chairs to allow her feet to touch the floor. Her wide feet were encased in scampers slit at the front to enable a comfortable fit. She wore these to receptions by University Presidents and visiting dignitaries, and was never fazed by "fashion." That's the understatement of the year! She "ran up" all her own dresses, all of them made from the same basic pattern. The family gave her an automatic washing machine for her 50th wedding anniversary, only to discover that two days later she had traded it in for a downstairs toilet. "I really needed that," she said.

My daughter Jean tells of playing Chinese checkers with her Grandma, and at age eight at the time, she usually lost. My mother never succumbed to the idea that she should pander to her granddaughter.

I have a photo of her in long fashionable skirts, paddling a canoe on a lake near Banff in 1917. Nothing, however, prepared her adequately for her first canoe trips with my Dad. Her version says they paddled from Point-au-Baril to Manitoulin Island and back, eating beans, beans, and more beans for meals. However she soon got into the swing of it, and by the time I was born, the family had been canoeing and tenting for the summer months on various lakes: Nipigon, Shebandowan, Lake of the Woods, and Superior. I was taken along at three months in a tikinagan complete with moss diapers. Our canoe was a twenty foot freighter, five feet in the beam with two sets of oars and seven paddles. Nine people. The load was so high (we packed food for the month) and as my mother couldn't see my father in the stern, they communicated by shouting at the top of their lungs. To change places, they rolled on their stomachs over the high load. We experienced lots of rain and wind and raging storms when we had to hold the tent down with our bodies. "Blow, winds, and crack your cheeks! rage! blow!"[2]

My father was careful about the weather, and especially on Lake Superior

---

2   William Shakespeare, *King Lear* (3.2.1).

trips, we had to get up at dawn "to beat the wind" and were usually camped by ten in the morning. However I can remember twice when we couldn't sight land because of the vastness of Lake Superior. And on one occasion, the swells from the large lake freighters almost swamped us, and mother yelled her indignation because sitting in the bow, she had shipped a bit of water. We were never shipwrecked, but had a feel for what it might be like.

She excelled at opening her home for hospitality. After United Church Ordination services in Winnipeg, the house would be crowded with theological students and their families, drinking coffee and eating her homemade donuts until all hours of the morning. When a friend, Ken Cash, was deathly sick and needed care, she set up a bed in the living room and nursed him. There was an endless stream of single men to our house, who, in retrospect, were seeking hospitality and understanding for their sexual orientation. Any and all United Church missionaries and their families from northern Manitoba or elsewhere could always find a bed and a welcome. When A.B.B. Moore, (see p. 157 of this book) spoke of my mother's home, he told me he thought at first it was an immigration shed!

As we could not determine the exact text that was used at her funeral, Dorothy Wyman, a lifelong friend, suggested that the following text suited Mother perfectly,

> *But before very long a fierce wind, the "North-easter" as they call it, tore down from the landward side. It caught the ship and, as it was impossible to keep head to wind, we had to give way and run before it...For days on end there was no sign of either sun or stars, a great storm was raging, and our last hopes of coming through alive began to fade...When day broke ... they noticed a bay with a sandy beach, on which they planned, if possible, to run the ship ashore...but [breakers] ran the ship aground...the stern was...pounded to pieces by the breakers...the centurion gave orders that those who could swim should jump overboard first and get to land; the rest were to follow, some on planks, some on parts of the ship....thus all came safely to land. Once we had made our way to safety we identified the island as Malta. The rough islanders treated us with uncommon kindness: because it was cold and had started to rain, they lit a bonfire and made us all welcome....the chief magistrate of the island ... took us in and entertained us hospitably for three days.*
> (Acts 27.14–16, 20, 39, 41, 44; 28.1, 2, 7 NEB)

This text appropriately reflects my mother's love of the water, combined with her generous hospitality to strangers. She would have resonated with Paul's experience. When she saw a fierce wind and rainstorm coming down the lake, she would have us pull to the shore, empty the canoe, and crawl under it to keep dry until the storm passed.

The Bible is filled with exhortations to hospitality. Psalm 23 speaks of it as being foundational to Bedouin culture, even "in the presence of my enemies." It is easy to entertain friends, but the entire Hebrew Bible calls us to receive the stranger into our midst. There is that memorable text,

> *It is he who sees justice done for the orphan and the widow, who loves the stranger and gives him food and clothing. Love the stranger then, for you were strangers in the land of Egypt."* (Deuteronomy 10.18-20 Jerusalem Bible)

The Greek Bible echoes that theme. "I was a stranger and you welcomed me," said Jesus in Matthew 25.35 (NRSV) when speaking of distinguishing the sheep from the goats. Romans 12.13 (NRSV) places hospitality to strangers among the highest virtues.

My mother practiced hospitality *par excellence.* How can hospitality be practiced beyond speaking to strangers at the coffee hour in your church? What supports can you extend to refugees newly arrived in this country? Temporary migrant workers? Filipino nannies far from home? What measures will you take to support a reliable, open, welcoming policy for refugees in Canadian government initiatives? The Roma from Hungary? The Muslims or Buddhists who come as new immigrants struggling with language, finances, loneliness?

ROBIN NEIL GIBSON, CANADA

1953 – 27 December 1998

Carpenter and joiner; Ecumenical advocate for rights of refugees; Staff for Asia development work for Anglican Church of Canada; Board of Inter-Church Act (six Canadian churches) for International Development; Chair of Consultative committee on Human Rights for Canadian Council of Churches; Director of The Primate's World Relief and Development Fund, an international development agency of the Anglican Church ('93–'98) for emergencies; Relief; Poverty; Monitored elections South Africa; Humanitarian concerns; Educator and advocate for change. Died of cancer at age 45.

Sri Lanka was engulfed in civil war. Svend Robinson, an NDP MP noted for his histrionic actions, was threatening to swim or wade across the crocodile infested waters dividing the Jaffna Peninsula from the rest of Sri Lanka, in order to reach the outpost of the battered Tamil population forced into that isolation by the harsh military Government. Only the intervention of a Conservative MP of the delegation offering to accompany him and therefore share the spotlight on this venture deterred him. Robin Gibson balanced all these personalities skillfully as staff of the eight days Canadian Human Rights Mission to Sri Lanka in January 1992. Sponsored by CIDA and The Department of External Affairs, it included several people from the churches and voluntary sector. This included myself as well as the Human Rights persons from all three political parties of the day. Guided by Robin, upon returning to Canada we delivered a first-hand account of our analysis of the human rights situation in Sri Lanka to the Canadian Government.

Robin was skilled in cultivating and nurturing human relationships as well as defending human rights. I think he must have learned some of that through his work as a carpenter—a "joiner" of the various parts that needed to be fit together to allow the "whole" to function properly, whether of things or of people. And we certainly needed those skills on that trip! A sensitive, capable, loving person, he coupled his practical experience as a "joiner" with his wide range of international and development experience gained over a period of years working in human rights and international development for the ecumenical community. His premature death came as a shock to everyone who had known him. He had this passage read at his funeral:

> *The spirit of the Lord God is upon me because the Lord has anointed me;he has sent me to bring good news to the humble, to bind up the broken-hearted; to proclaim liberty to captives and release to those in prison; to proclaim a year of the Lord's favour, and a day of vengeance of our God; to comfort all who mourn, to give them garlands instead of ashes, oil of gladness instead of mourners' tears; a garment of splendour for the heavy heart. They shall be called Trees of Righteousness, planted by the Lord for his glory. Ancient ruins shall be rebuilt and sites long desolate restored; they shall repair the ruined cities and restore what has long lain desolate.* (Isaiah 61.1–4 NEB)

What an appropriate text for one who spent his entire international ministry focusing not only on structural inequities that robbed persons of their potential, but also on such minutiae as the poor man in Nicaragua who needed an interest free bank loan to start up a motorcycle repair shop; the young lad in Brazil condemned by birth to live in the "favella" overlooking the tourist resort of Copacabana Beach; the weary Roma refugee from Hungary seeking safety in Canada; the young teenager in Soweto, South Africa, whose human rights were denied by his country for so many years. This was the kind of liberating work he did for the Anglican Church of Canada.

The Isaiah text speaks to this situation and tells of the stunning coming reversal of the fortunes in the God who liberates and delivers freedom. But note, as does theologian Walter Brueggemann on whose commentary I draw, that the first few verses uttered by his poet/visionary emphasize the actions of a "human agent"[3] to bring about this transformation of public life and a new regime according to the will of God. The visionary is empowered by the Spirit of God—that same spirit that breathed upon Creation. Brueggemann draws attention to the powerful action verbs that are used in this passage to enliven the human agent: "to bring," "to bind up," "to proclaim," "to release," "to proclaim," "to comfort," "to provide," "to give."[4]

Moreover, the "good news" mentioned in this passage is not for individuals only. It is not just for the broken hearted relatives of the twenty-six people massacred at the Sandy Hook Elementary School in Newton, Connecticut on 14 Dec. 2012. It is also for the entire community of Sandy Hook. It speaks of the restoration of ruined cities, and of desolate sites restored. Deliverance by God is an enormous social public event having implications for the organization of life together in the public space.

This glorious vision of hope will free the alienated and the marginalized to participate in a newly transformed public community where peace, prosperity, and safety abound. Unrealistic? It is, after all, a vision, not a reality, but a vision not without its awareness of economic realities such as the gap between the rich and the poor. The text evokes the "year of the Lord's favour." This refers to Leviticus 25, the "Year of Jubilee," when in Hebrew tradition, economic transactions were to take place so all would again be on a level playing field. In 2000, Canadian churches mounted the "Jubilee campaign," pressing Western governments to forgive the debts of the most heavily indebted countries. Here is a vision of the "good news" as transformation of social and economic relationships between the haves and the have-nots.[5]

When Jesus quoted this text in his first sermon (Luke 4.18-19), the people of Nazareth found the "gospel" so radical that they threatened to throw him over the hill and kill him. They didn't like the implication that the good news meant a re-ordering of economic relationships, and they rejected both the message and the messenger. Has the contemporary church lost that cutting edge message?

---

3   Walter Brueggemann, *Isaiah 40-66*, pp. 212-13.
4   Walter Brueggemann, *Isaiah 40-66*, p. 213.
5   See the entries on Garth Legge (p. 36) and Maria Theresa Porcile Santiso (p. 48) in this book.

The United Church is very strong condemning discrimination or abuse of persons because of gender, age, or race. Robin's ministry targeted all human rights abuses, including structural economic ones that manifest themselves in class disparity. The screen saver on his computer was "Justice, not Just Us." This issue may be even harder than any of the others, because it strikes at what many people would consider their privacy in our culture. In India, the first question I was asked was, "How much money do you make?" I felt as if I had been assaulted. It was the equivalent of being asked by a stranger here in Canada about my sexual history. How long are we going to resist the clear gospel imperative that requires structural economic changes in our situation?

But there was another string to Robin's bow. I was impressed, when at Robin's funeral at St James Cathedral in Toronto, a pick-up choir of his friends led the singing so beautifully. And I was even more impressed when the song of the Bridegroom to his beloved from Song of Songs was read alongside the passage from Isaiah. No one else I know of had ever chosen this passage to be read at their funeral:

> *Wear me as a seal upon your heart, as a seal upon your arm; for love is strong as death, passion cruel as the grave; it blazes up like blazing fire, fiercer than any flame. Many waters cannot quench love, no flood can sweep it away; if a man were to offer for love the whole wealth of his house, it would be utterly scorned.*
> (Song of Songs 8.6–7 NEB)

What a great affirmation of the fulfillment of creation in human sexuality in all its aspects. Who of us would choose such a text for our funeral? Obviously sexual identity and passionate love for his partner was part of Robin's self-understanding of what it means to be fully human. Would that the church at large, in its theology, practices, children's stories, liturgies and rituals, embrace such an affirmation joyously and unreservedly. One step along the way has been the United Church's support for same sex couples, gays, lesbians and transgendered persons and the congregations who joyously affirm such a stance. We badly need a robust theology of sexuality for heterosexual persons as well, in a sex-drenched world where sexual relationships have been so crudely distorted and commercialized.

JOHN GARDNER HARVEY, CANADA
April 1952 – 22 February 1994

Horticulturalist; Educated University of Guelph, ON; Graduated in Agriculture; Worked at Hamilton Botanical Gardens and Scientific advisor to staff of Chapman Agricultural Chemicals. Sailor; My nephew and one of five children; Photographer, musician, artist; Married to Elaine (died '91) and then Rinette. One son, Trevor. Died prematurely of cardiomyopathy.

Summer 1952. There were the three of them in dresser drawers provided by my mother at the family home in Winnipeg. (Why buy cribs when the babies would outgrow them in the flash of an eye?) My nephews Chris Freeman and John Harvey and my daughter Ruth had all been born about the same time in the early months of 1952. We were all so excited to have the three babies together at my mother's home in Winnipeg.

Later they went their separate ways. Chris became an expert in conflict management and mediation; Ruth a family practice doctor; and John a horticulturist. He knew trouble and sorrow. He lost his first wife Elaine through her early death, and he struggled all his short life to cope with the diagnosis of cardiomyopathy that robbed his second wife Rinette, of her newly minted husband. When a new heart finally became available, it was too late. None of this prevented him from becoming a first-class sailor, nor from enjoying life to the fullest extent possible. He loved growing things, and he loved sending people information as to how to do just that. His sister Margaret still has a book, *Urban Garden*, that was a Christmas present from him. He was a proud father, and spent an inordinate amount of time fashioning a Halloween costumes for his son Trevor for the school party. But in the words of his sister Margaret, he died "waaaaaaaay too early in life."

His premature early death at age forty and his short life were honoured at his funeral when Psalm 103 was read by my daughter Jean. It is a long psalm, beginning with a paean of praise for the steadfastness of God's love: the utter reliability of the One who "pardons," "heals," "rescues," "surrounds," and "contents," as theologian Walter Brueggemann points out. What more can one ask? The psalm goes on to address both the human's guilt and mortality. I quote in particular those verses addressing our mortality, since John had died at such an early age.

> *As a father has compassion on his children, so has the Lord compassion on all who fear him. For he knows how we were made, he knows full well that we are dust. Man's days are like the grass; he blossoms like the flowers of the field: a wind passes over them, and they cease to be, and their place knows them no more. But the Lord's love never fails those that fear him; his righteousness never fails their sons and their grandsons who listen to his voice and keep his covenant, who remembers his commandments and obey them.* (Psalm 103.13–18 NEB)

How appropriate to read a psalm that links the compassion of the Father with the fragile and dependent human being as dust, referring to the moment of Creation itself as in Genesis 2.7 (NEB). As a horticulturist, John worked with the soil and the plants and the flowers of the field. His life work was to tend the earth and coax its bountiful riches to life. He knew how to create the conditions that promoted growth in the dust and the earth, but insisted that the responsible use of chemicals in agriculture was essential to growth. This stance was not undisputed by his siblings. But his death reminded all of us of the fragility of human existence, and of our utter dependence on the breath of life, given by the Creator, to be a living being.

What does this text mean for us? Among many implications, surely one is to raise the question as to what can be done about the impending collapse of the environment. Some years ago, when the United Church announced its boycott of bottled water, a member of the church I attended exploded, "It's just one more dumb thing that gives the United Church a bad name!" I think not. Water is the oil of the twenty-first century. The battle is now on as to whether water is a commodity that can be sold to the highest bidder, or whether water is a gift of God and should be available to all on a needs basis.

Already the Empire (by which I mean the collusion of economic and political interests worldwide) is putting its policies in place. The corporate sector, in close alliance with the World Bank and the International Monetary, has turned water into a tradable profitable economic product to be owned, exploited, marketed and sold to the highest bidder. In Bolivia the privatization of the water system, which was a condition of receiving a loan from the World Bank, doubled the price of water. An Argentinean businessman is reported to have earned a profit of one hundred million dollars on a privatized water deal. Bottled water is now a thirty-three billion dollar annual business.

The problem is the uneven distribution of water, the exclusion of access to clean water for millions of people (notably the indigenous peoples in Canada), and the accumulation of millions of dollars for a small minority of people. Isn't it time that Christians took a long hard look at this situation, and began to bring their best theological analysis to the public debate? Isn't it time we reconsidered the meaning of the Genesis 1.27-29 (NEB) statement:

> *So God created...male and female... and said to them, "... fill the earth and subdue it, rule over the fish of the sea, the birds of heaven, and every living thing that moves upon the earth?"*

Is this the misused theological rationale for our perceived superiority rights above other life forms?

For indigenous people the entire cosmos is sacred community and life should be lived with respect for the sacred. Theirs is a sacramental vision of life that has been largely discarded by modernity. Mary Jamieson, a Mohawk member of the '98 Canadian Federal panel assessing the environmental impact of the burial of nuclear waste in the Laurentian Shield, exploded at one session, "You have stolen our rivers, our lakes, our land. We will not allow you to take our rocks as well. We will not allow you to bury toxic nuclear waste in our rocks. I never used to believe this but now I do. Rocks are alive."

Jeanette Armstrong, Director of the Canada Research Chair for the Sylix

Okanagan First Nations Communities and an aboriginal poet and leader, raises questions about the meaning of trees in different cultures. "To someone from the lumber industry, the word tree has a significantly different meaning than to an orchardist. To a person whose direct survival depends upon trees, the 'tree' has a deeper cultural meaning steeped in an essence of gratitude toward the creation of the trees and therefore enveloped within a unique cultural expression of reverence toward creation. Consider the extreme difference between a logging conglomerate president's meaning and one in whose culture 'trees' are living relatives in spirit. Perhaps it is time to learn the meaning of trees."[6]

The slogan of Liberation theologians from Latin America, which used to be "God's preferential option for the poor," has now become "God's preferential option for the earth." The earth is the new poor, and it is screaming that it has had enough of abuse and exploitation.

The Orthodox churches have built into their liturgy an acknowledgment of the sanctity of Creation. Part of the ritual of the Feast of the Epiphany is the "Blessing of the Waters," which usually takes place outside near a stream or river. It is a ritual to help us recognize that all of God's Creation can be transformed by God's sacramental presence. God is recognized as transcendent and immanent simultaneously, and this liturgical celebration calls us to repentance for our abuse of Creation.

Some believe that the earth exists for us and we can manage its resources for our own benefit as we wish. Ironically commerce, masquerading as liberation, has become one of the most prominent forms of "dominion theology." Canada will now subsidize its mining companies in the Congo, for example, under the guise of elevating the standard of living of the Congolese.

The theme of fragility is echoed in the hymn "Praise, My Soul, the God of Heaven," which says, "Frail as summer's flower we flourish; blows the wind and it is gone" (VU #240). Do we not need to balance the small accomplishments of our own lives with the knowledge that those who share our commitment to the earthh and who come after us will carry on the struggle? To honour John Harvey is for us to gain strength from his dedication to the care of the plants, the flowers, the vegetables, the soil itself as he coaxed beauty from the earth, and to carry on that work in our time. That's what the communion of saints is all about isn't it?

---

6   Unpublished address to a WCC consultation in Toronto, about 1985.

Arthur Bruce Barbour Moore, Canada
4 February 1906 – 9 September 2004

Educator; Ecumenist; Minister of United Church of Canada and its Moderator ('70–'72); Born Keswick Ridge, New Brunswick; Celtic stock; Son of Congregationalist minister; Educated in Eastern Townships, McGill University, Montreal, and Oxford; Minister in churches in Quebec, Ontario, and Saskatchewan; Principal St Andrews Theological College, Saskatoon ('46–'50); President and Vice Chancellor Victoria University, University of Toronto ('50–'70); Chancellor University of Toronto ('77–'80); Order of Canada ('76). Married to Margaret; children and grandchildren.

"She will enter ministry through the kitchen door," Dr. A.B.B. Moore said of me at the '50 Spring Theological Convocation in Winnipeg. I had earned my B.D. degree along with my male counterparts preparing for ordained ministry, and was planning on marriage in a month's time. Although Moore came from a Congregationalist tradition that had ordained women in the USA as early as the last 1880s, he knew that in 1950 it looked as though there was no future for married women in ordered United Church ministry. In 1928 the United Church declared that "there was no bar in religion or reason to the ordination of women to the ministry." But there were plenty of others, not the least of which were cultural assumptions about the proper role of women, informed by a patriarchal culture that dominated decision making in Canada at the time. The prevailing sentiment was that married women would not be able to "give themselves wholly" to ministry because of the demands of children and husband. For single women, there was no problem. At the 1962 General Council only one recommendation was adopted by the General Council on this matter. Ordination would be open to "those women who were unmarried or were widows or were at that time in life when they were no longer required in the home as mothers." Female ordination would be considered if a suitable ministry could be arranged that did not interfere with "the stability of the marriage and their position as wives." My husband Roy was one of sixty-two men and women who insisted their negative votes be recorded. The debate raged on. The '64 General Council lifted its restrictions on the ordination of married women, and I, the mother of four under twelve years of age, was ordained in 1965 with full support of the congregation, Roy, and A.B.B. Moore. It was a tribute to the flexibility and forward looking vision of the leaders and members of the United Church—the first mainline church in Canada to do so.

A.B.B. (as he was known) was the son of a Congregationalist minister, who at age twenty-one witnessed the birth of the United Church. He brought a certain independence and nonconformist tradition to that union. For him, the new church was to become a key force in Canadian nation building. He supported that phrase in the Basis of Union that states, "It shall be the policy of the United Church to foster the spirit of unity in the hope that this sentiment of ministry may in due time, so far as Canada is concerned, take shape in a church which may be fittingly be described as national." He was a close friend of nationalist Prime Minister Mike Pearson, whose funeral tribute, delivered by then Moderator A.B.B. Moore, was as follows: "Compounded of devotion and intelligence, of persistence and sensitivity, of humour and courage, of vision and practicality, he was a great human being."

A.B.B.'s significant contributions to the "religious, ecumenical and educational life" of Canadians were recognized in 1976 when he received the Order of Canada. As the '71–'72 Moderator of the United Church and an ecumenist, this towering man co-chaired the Commission on Union with the Anglican Church, although this proposal ultimately failed. As President of Victoria University, he was involved in the formation of the Toronto School of Theology (TST), an ecumenical consortium for graduate theological students. After some years of blood, sweat and tears, the formal agreement was signed in

1970 during his final year as President. To this day it includes seven theological colleges from the Roman Catholic, Anglican and Reformed traditions and affiliated colleges in Ontario, and is home to students from age 20-80 from sixty-two countries. It is the largest of its kind in Canada.

During his tenure as President of Victoria University in Toronto, (where he was referred to as a legend), he expanded the campus and contributed to its educational effectiveness by helping to found the EJ Pratt Library, the Margaret Addison Hall, and the Northrop Frye Hall. All of these resources continue to serve contemporary students.

He was a person of great humility and warmth .The last time I saw him at a public gathering was at the General Council of 2000 in Toronto. He was then 94, and a car had been sent to transport him for the Opening Service. I happened to live near him, and so was included in that arrangement. On the return trip that night, he suddenly said, "That is a church I no longer recognize." No wonder. Due to scorching weather, most delegates were charging around in shorts and T-shirts—a far cry from the black gowned formality of an earlier day. No Prime Minister or Premier came with greetings to that gathering. The music was unfamiliar. Yet he continued to support the church he no longer recognized with all his strength and prayers.

I have his name in my Bible opposite Psalm 23, which was read at his funeral. Because I have commented on that Psalm elsewhere, I have chosen to use a text that typifies the life of A.B.B. Moore as the forward looking leader that I knew. After Moses had experienced the presence of God in the burning bush, God charges him with confronting Pharaoh and then bringing the Israelites out of Egyptian captivity.

> *Then Moses said to God, "If I go to the Israelites and tell them that the God of their forefathers has sent me to them, and they ask me his name, what shall I say?" God answered, "I AM; that is who I am. Tell them I AM has sent you to them." And God said further, "You must tell the Israelites that it is Jehovah, the God of their forefathers, the God of Abraham, the God of Isaac, the God of Jacob, who has sent you to them. This is my name forever; this is my title in every generation."*
>
> (Exodus 3.13-15 NEB)

This phrase "I AM; that is who I am" is more correctly translated as "I will be what I will be."[7] It is a phrase indicating movement and progression. God's identity is bound up with change, transformation, renewal, and newness. The "I AM" is the Liberator. This is the God who liberates the oppressed from slavery in Egypt and from oppression in Babylon. This is the God who continues to disclose his identity. I remember Marga Bührig, President of the WCC (see p. 12 of this book), emphasizing this very point in one of our theological exchanges at a WCC Executive meeting that threatened to become bogged down in status quo business matters.

When Jesus spoke to the Pharisees outside the temple treasury (John 7 and 8), the disclosure of God's identity continued. In defending the validity of his testimony, Jesus told them in effect that they have no knowledge of the God who liberates those who suffer, and who is qualitatively different from the one they worship. "I am from above," he said (John 8.23 Jerusalem Bible). "I do nothing on my own, but I speak these things as the Father instructed me" (John 8.28 NRSV). Jesus claimed to be in continuity with that same One who spoke to Moses, and who continues to disclose the true mission and nature of I AM as Liberator. The disclosure of God's identity continues. God is the Liberator of the blind, the poor, the prisoner, the broken victims, the foreigner, the widow and orphan, and of all who suffer. Jesus' claim "I AM from above" spoke to the ongoing process of divulging and revealing the Liberator in new situations of oppression. This theological understanding is expressed in the New Creed of the United Church of Canada in the line, "We believe in God: who has created and is creating" (VU p. 918).

Although A.B.B. Moore did not recognize the new body of Christ in all its strange and different manifestations and practices, he continued to support it and pray for it. He was a man who always looked to the future, and he trusted the wisdom, discernment and faithfulness of those who now sought to embody the mission of liberation in a new form.

How do we understand this text for God's mission in our context? Who can help us with this discernment? Who are the suffering ones in your circle of friends and acquaintances? Who are the suffering ones beyond your circle? What does liberation mean for them? You can't do it all, so what will be your priority? What about the rich and the middle class? From what do they need liberation? What will be your first action? In what sense will you understand this to be part of God's mission?

---

7   See footnote to Exodus 3.14 in the NEB.

BARTON (BART) LOUIS PAGEL, USA

15 January 1937 – 18 December 2002

Businessman with Bechtel Corporation; Manager of Project Control for the Trans-Alaska Pipeline; Human Resources, Kaiser Permanente (10 years); Son of a Lutheran lay minister; Presbyterian; Joined US Navy ('50); Installed first computer system for Naval Air Station in Alameda; Former US Navy Commander; Sailor; sportsman; Multiple hobbies; Stoic; Risk taker; Sensitive gentle-man; Lover of all things English, including antiques, unassuming. Father of four, married to Diana "Di" Phillips.

I met Bart when I occupied the Chair of Contemporary Theology at Lafayette-Orinda Presbyterian Church, California, for six weeks in 1994. He loved sailing and had purchased a 35 foot sailboat, *H.M.S. Bold Venture*, which he sailed in San Francisco Bay. The story is told of how he had once donated a free sail on the bay and lunch for a school auction. Bart's sister-in-law Nancy went along with the two families who had won the trip, none of whom knew how to sail. In extremely rough water near the Golden Gate Bridge, Bart saw a man who had been knocked off his windsurfing board, calling for help. Because of the turbulent weather, the boom came around and knocked Bart overboard. Nancy was trapped on one side and the rest were down below. Bart had managed to grab a piece of bumper rope, and although the boat was careening wildly, he managed to claw his way back, climbed back into the boat and grabbed the tiller. "We've got to go back to rescue that man," he shouted. By then a Coast Guard boat was on the way to rescue the windsurfer and Bart's *Bold Venture* was not needed. Nevertheless he had tried, and the story was indicative of this kind and courageous man.

Faith was important to him, and nothing could deter him from attending church, where the music was very special to him. He was definitely confident in his own person, and never thought too highly of himself. I could never discern ego demands to be noticed, or to be first, or dominant. In short, he was one of "the salt of the earth." Here is the Psalm that was read at his funeral.

> *O Lord, my heart is not proud, nor are my eyes haughty; I do not busy myself with great matters or things too marvelous for me. No; I submit myself, I account myself lowly, as a weaned child clinging to its mother. O Israel, look for the Lord now and evermore.* (Psalm 131 NEB)

This psalm was unknown to me, but singularly appropriate for Bart Pagel, who was completely at home in this world, who knew his limitations, and was entirely content with doing tasks close at hand and manageable for him. He trusted in God's motherly care (as illustrated in the lino cut on p. 161), and practiced that trust in the ordinary routine events of everyday life. He was at ease with himself and willing to submit to his Creator in his relationship as creature. His strength was evident in the fight he put up against the heart disease that claimed his life. He was not vying for fame or fortune. He was someone to whom the term "gentle-man" really applied.

This text is a good antidote and balance for those who admire "busy, busy churches" and churches with tons of activities every week. Although they may offer many commendable activities, Jesus seldom gets a mention, and is crowded out by "busyness." Since I have retired, the conversation with other retirees frequently centres on how busy we are, and how we don't know how we had time for our work before we retired. Busyness is viewed as a very positive quality to exhibit in one's life. Not to be busy is seen as indolence. When my husband Roy retired, he indicated that he would sit in a rocking chair, and in a few years, he might even begin to rock. "I'm going to be," he said. This psalm has something important to say about busying ourselves with things "too marvelous" for us. And here is the paradox of the gospel that calls us to creative engagement and discipleship, but also to "active waiting."

Ponder this additional text that was read at Bart's funeral:

> *Comfort, comfort, my people; it is the voice of your God; speak tenderly to Jerusalem and tell her this, that she has fulfilled her term of bondage, that her penalty is paid; she has received at the Lord's hand double measure for all her sins. There is a voice that cries: Prepare a road for the Lord through the wilderness, clear a highway across the desert for our God. Every valley shall be lifted up, every mountain and hill brought down; rugged places shall be made smooth and the mountain-ranges become a plain. Thus shall the glory of the Lord be revealed, and all mankind together shall see it; for the Lord himself has spoken. A voice says, "Cry"; and another asks, "What shall I cry?" "That all mankind is grass; they last no longer than a flower of the field. The grass withers, the flower fades, when the breath of the Lord blows upon them; the grass withers, the flowers fade, but the word of our God endures for evermore." You who bring Zion good news, up with you to the mountain top; lift up your voice and shout, you who bring good news to Jerusalem, up, lift it up fearlessly, cry to the cities of Judah, "Your God is here!"* (Isaiah 40.1–9 NEB)

What a joyous text for his funeral, and also for the faith community! The passage addresses the situation of the people of Israel who, after a long civil war and the destruction of their Temple in Jerusalem, had been carried off into exile in Babylon. The text confidently predicts that the Israelite exiles will return to their home, and even built a Second Temple. This text celebrates the "good news" (or "gospel")[8] of that homecoming. The mention of "good news" in verse nine, that God always opens up "new possibilities,"[9] is the first use of this term in the Hebrew Bible. Here again is struck that note of confidence in the reliability of God, so appropriate for Bart.

But the new possibilities come at a price. There will be a vast upheaval. I have never understood how we can join in a Sing-along-Messiah, which is this sacred text set to glorious music year after year, as a more-or-less popular seasonal song. Are we aware of what we are singing? Do we notice that this text understands God's action as turning things upside down? Valleys will rise up. Mountains will go down. The entire landscape will look and be different. Would we sing it with such fervour if we knew it meant the equivalent of an earthquake in our lives? That it implies a change in the shape and appearance of the believing community?

---

8 Walter Brueggemann, *Isaiah 40–66*, pp. 11–12.
9 Walter Brueggemann, *Isaiah 40–66*, p. 16.

The upheaval promises new possibilities which will overcome our fatigue and restore our energies. Life is worthwhile after all. So much in our world is transitory; our brief lives are like the withering grass or the fading flowers and seem meaningless. In contrast, the poem speaks of the presence of God that endures. The big "parade," to use Brueggemann's term,[10] signaling God's decisive return, brings enduring comfort after the suffering and upheaval of the exile and the desert existence. It gives a lie to the "And there is none to comfort" of Lamentations. A wide highway will be opened up across the desert, anticipating the triumphal return of God. Find someone to tell about this parade, shouts the poet. "Up with you to the mountain top; lift up your voice and shout," the good news of God's enduring presence. Look who is finally back in town. Let's sing! That is the kind of homecoming it will be.

But the best thing about the good news is that the homecoming and the new possibilities are for everybody. The verb "comfort" is plural, and invites all "my people" to participate in God's covenant made previously with David. It is not just for the suffering exiles returning home from Babylon, nor just for members of the United Church. It's also for the guys sleeping on downtown pavements. It is not just for Christians. It is a democratization of the covenant, echoing God's recognition of the "outsider," in this case the Persian Cyrus as one of God's instruments. What a scandalous notion! How disgraceful! You mean that deliverance, hope, even "salvation" may come through an unexpected peripheral agent? Through those unfocused kids in the Occupy movement? Or those aboriginal peoples in the Idle No More Movement and not through church resolutions? Or through the Christians of the Global South and desperate developing countries, whom we assume need us to build schools for them? Or through the lakes and forests, oceans and earth itself, that are collapsing under the very heavy blows we have dealt them?

Some ask what the future United Church of Canada will look like. This text is our story as well as that of the ancient Israelites, and it assures us God is reliable in keeping promises of "homecoming" to a faithful people. Bart knew that. But the landscape will be very different from the familiar one we know. And the transformation of that landscape into something entirely unrecognizable, but beautiful, may come through unexpected sources. Pray that we may be open to "homecoming" when it appears.

---

10 Walter Brueggemann, *Isaiah 40–66*, pp. 18.

Margaret Evelyn Prang, Canada

23 January 1921 – 12 January 2013

Educator; Professor of History at UBC ('57–'86); Social democrat; Agnostic Christian; Feminist; Manitoba SCM and United College, Winnipeg ('46); PhD in History, University of Toronto; Hon. Degree LLD from University of Winnipeg and UBC; Queen's Silver Jubilee Medal; Love-Hate relationship with the United Church of Canada; Camper on Georgian Bay and Galiano Island, BC; Mother of Charlene and Carmen, grandmother of Justin.

At a time in Canadian history when single women were denied the privilege of adopting a child, she became one of the first single women in BC to do so, and her commitment to her daughters and grandson are legendary. Her adoption of Charlene was an historic landmark in Canada. She was an innovator and a pioneer in developing a new concept of family which did not necessarily include a husband.

By her own definition, she was an agnostic Christian, meaning that she didn't have all the answers to the mystery of life, and preferred to raise questions and air doubts, when others hesitated. She continued to raise troublesome questions about Christian faith and the church throughout her life, including her professorial career at the University of British Columbia. Yet she attended church faithfully. Her inquiring mind, self-deprecating sense of humour, and intellectual energy gave many permission to openly air their doubts about the faith. She never allowed facile certitude to masquerade as faith. She left instructions about her funeral, among which a quote from Martin Buber was, "Faith is keeping an open mind about mystery." She lived not by certainty but by informed faith.

I first met her in Winnipeg in 1944 when we were students and active in the Student Christian Movement (SCM.) Subsequently, she was a staff member of the SCM in Britain and in Canada. A few years ahead of me, she was one whom we counted on for intellectual rigour, an open inquisitive mind, and a profound questioning of Christian faith and of everything else! I remember asking her if she thought history was a linear affair that just went on and on, or was it circular? No definitive answer from her spurred me on to do my own thinking. So she was obviously a good teacher.

She was also a superb scholar with an interest in political and constitutional history. Her attention to social and intellectual history became evident as she won the UBC medal for popular biography in 1975 with the publication of her book, *N.W. Rowell: Ontario Nationalist*, father of Mary Rowell Jackman, one of the saints I write about in this book. Newton Rowell was a leading Methodist layman in the church union debates of 1925, central to the famous 1929 "Persons Case," which recognized women legally as persons and secured the right of Canadian women to sit in the Senate. He was in the forefront of many major political and social reform movements of the early 20th century. This landmark book resulted in Margaret's election as president of the Canadian Historical Association in 1976-77.

She also chose the Biblical texts that were to be read at her service. They were Luke 17.20-24 ("The Kingdom of God is among you"); John 1.1-9 ("In the beginning was the Word"); and Isaiah 40.25-31 ("They shall rise up with wings, as eagles"). The first two texts were not chosen by any other person for any funeral that I have ever known, and the choice reflects Margaret's independent and inquiring spirit and mind.

They are all so appropriate for Margaret. At her funeral, the minister Brian Thorpe spoke about the first text: "In fact," says Jesus, 'the kingdom of God is among you.' Margaret has taught us that the kingdom is defined by humility and curiosity in the midst of great mystery, intellectual rigour, delight in creation, humour and great love. What a gift! Thanks be." The second text, from John, is Margaret's theological statement as to what she believed life and the gospel are all about. Here it is.

> *In the beginning was the Word, and the Word was with God, and the Word was God. He was in the beginning with God. All things came into being through him, and without him not one thing came into being. What has come into being in him was life, and the life was the light of all people. The light shines in the darkness, and the darkness did not overcome it. There was a man sent from God, whose name was John. He came as a witness to testify to the light, so that all might believe through him. He himself was not the light, but he came to testify to the light. The true light, which enlightens everyone, was coming into the world...And the Word became flesh and lived among us, and we have seen his glory, the glory of a father's only son, full of grace and truth.* (John 1.1-9, 14 NRSV)

Trust Margaret to steer clear of any sentimentality or platitudes. The John passage underlines the central Christian belief in the Incarnation: "the Word became flesh and lived among us." Ours is not a disembodied faith. The material and spiritual are not separate entities. The earthly man Jesus is for us a window into God. Jesus reveals God as compassionate, forgiving, loving and merciful, and in that sense was a prism through which we see the divine. He also reveals for us the best a human being can become. But the Incarnation goes beyond that understanding. "I began to understand God's becoming human no longer as a unique, completed event, but as an ongoing process in history. In this process God is rendered invisible (as in Auschwitz), or is made manifest in the experiences of liberation."[11] In that sense, we are involved in the ongoing manifestation of the holy by our actions.

The text continues. "We have seen his glory." The word "glory" is a comic word in Hebrew, having to do with bulk and weight. A fat person was one who was glorious. We still speak of a person "who carries a lot of weight" in a meeting. The word of such a person can be trusted because the whole self is behind it. That is, the person can produce results, or has a lot of power to produce results. The person's weight and presence shines through the words and actions. Here the reference is to the "glory of a father's only son," Jesus, who embodies the grace and truth of God.

"Only gradually did a certain expansion take place within my theological biography," writes theologian Dorothee Sölle, "from this strictly Christocentric position toward a reflection on the ground of life, on God. Today I am more

---

11 Dorothee Sölle, *Against the Wind*, p. 40.

and more aware of how necessary this is in encounters with other religions, for example, with Judaism and others who have been called not by Christ but, rather, by other voices of the God of many voices....Trying to speak another language...enables us to hear better. Indeed, for me Christ is God's clearest voice, but the meaning does not preclude other voices of the divine for other people, for example, Zen Buddhists. Not to understand this is to fall victim to religious imperialism."[12]

What is the meaning of the Incarnation for you? How does it inform your understanding and relationship to those of other living faiths?

---

12 Dorothee Söllee, *Against the Wind*, p. 34.

M.M. THOMAS, SOUTH INDIA
15 May 1916 – 3 December 1996

Ecumenist: Mar Thoma Syrian Church of Malabar, tracing its roots to St Thomas the Apostle (First century C.E.); Sec. Student Christian Movement (Madras,India); Youth Sec of Mar Thoma Church, India; staff of World Student Christian Federation, Geneva ('47–'52); Delegate to First Assembly of 1948 World Council of Churches n Amsterdam; Chair of WCC's Church and Society Department ('61–'68); Chaired World Conference on Church and Society, Geneva ('66); Chairman of Central Committee of WCC ('68–'75); Established the Christian Institute for the Study of Religion and Society, Kerala, South India ('57–'76); Wrote on social policy; Cultural encounter; Christian-Hindu relations; Political analysis; Ecumenism; Bible studies; Governor of Nagaland in North East India ('91); Guest professor at Princeton Seminary, USA ('80–'87); Three-year research project on mission and evangelism in India.

I became very anxious when I learned that M.M. Thomas—a theological giant and committed ecumenist would be in the Mar Thoma congregation, and I was to preach. I was on a three month visit to the Ecumenical Institute, Whitefield, South India, and had been offered as preacher on this occasion. But I was comforted by M.M.'s public claim that "theology was not so much a body of knowledge but a process that takes place in actual life situations, when those who live by faith in Jesus Christ seek to understand the character of the situation in which they are, and their function in it, in the light of that faith." Yes, I knew my sermon would try to reflect that understanding.

I had heard of M.M. Thomas, a member of the Mar Thoma Church, for years before I met him in Bangalore, India. I knew that he had been Moderator of the Central Committee of the World Council of Churches when the General assembly met in Madras in 1968, the first meeting of that body in Asia. My first trip to India (1975) was hosted by a priest of the Mar Thoma Church (M.A. Thomas—another Thomas!), and I was exposed to its rich Syrian Orthodox Liturgical tradition, and evangelical piety. The church claims roots to the apostle St Thomas who migrated to India and founded the Christian community and church which still bear his name.

M.M.'s work and writings were legendary in the ecumenical community worldwide. I knew that he had been influenced not only by his commitment to Christ, but also by both the Indian Independence Movement (Gandhi) and the Marxist movement, moving him from passive social work to political activism. I knew that he had applied for ordination in the Mar Thoma Church as well as membership in the Communist party. The Church rejected him because of his Marxism; Communists rejected him because of his Christian faith. I knew that he opposed Indira Gandhi's suspension of Indian democracy in 1976, and that he resigned his post as Governor of Nagaland in North East India in 1993 after two years, in protest against central government corruption. Here was a layman deeply committed to the struggle of the poor for justice, who became a self-educated theologian of note, a prolific writer on Christian ethics, and a Christian witness to a world in revolution.

When I enquired about the scripture used at his funeral, my friend Aruna Gnanadason put me in touch with her Indian colleague, Jesudas Athyal, who wrote, "In the Mar Thoma Church, the whole funeral service is highly liturgical. All the Bible readings are prescribed by the church, and there are separate readings for men, women, and children. The funeral service itself is in two parts—one at home and the other in the church—with two readings each. There is a list of these from which the pastor will choose one. For men the epistle will be either 1 Corinthians 15.35-58 or 1 Thessalonians 4.13-18, and the gospel portion would be either John 5.19-29 or John 11.20-27. No records are kept in the church for the readings of a particular service, which means that the only way to know the exact text is if the family had audio or video recorded the service."

Because I could not identify the exact text read at his funeral, I have chosen the following psalm which is a text I heard him elucidate, and which I most closely associate with this man. For him it was the focus of much of his work and ministry.

> *Happy are we whose sons in their early prime stand like tall towers, our daughters like sculptured pillars at the corners of a palace. Our barns are full and furnish plentiful provision; Our sheep bear lambs in thousands upon thousands; The oxen in our fields are fat and sleek; there is no miscarriage or untimely birth, No cried of distress in our public places. Happy are the people in such a case as ours; happy the people who have the Lord for their God.*
> (Psalm 144.12–15 NEB)

For him, this psalm points to signs of a "saved" society—a society where our common future is acted out together, in the light of our covenant with God. What are the signs of such a society?

Verse 12 is an affirmation of sex in all its romantic and erotic aspects, both in health of the body and beauty of form; verse 13 points to signs of economic prosperity and plenty. We might express it as industrial wealth in contemporary terms. It is emphatically a society where everyone has enough to eat. Verse 14 speaks of social security and social justice; of an end to aggression and disasters; of peace in our streets. And finally the psalm speaks of the covenant between God and people that makes this state of affairs possible: where creation has coherence and reliability because of a spiritual relationship between God and people. This was a central tenet of his life.

Not for M.M. an empty discussion about whether religion and politics mix. He was, after all, Governor of Nagaland in East India for a year or more. He would applaud Desmond Tutu who appeared at the 6th Assembly of the World Council of Churches in 1983, holding a Bible aloft for all to see, and declaring, "You brought us this book. Did you think we wouldn't read it?" It was a given for both of them that God's world encompasses every area of our lives: economics, politics, technology, arts, sports, and commerce. M.M. lived in a country where Christians were a minority, yet he made a significant contribution to the body politic in his country. He constantly interacted with Hindus, including Gandhi, as well as those active Communists who lived in his home state of Kerala. Later he broke with Communist ideology, and fully embraced Christian ecumenism and its witness in the world. His entire life was an attempt to discover and express what is involved in the intersection of Christian faith and ethics with those of other convictions living in a secular pluralistic society.

In the process, he interacted with other famed ecumenists in India from the Orthodox tradition such as Paulos Mar Gregorius (1922-96), Metropolitan of the Syrian Orthodox Church, whose beginnings in India date well before the 7th century. Paulos was not only a theologian who led his church into interfaith dialogue, but a first-rate ping pong player who defeated me at a game at which I thought I was unbeatable.

M.M.'s writings and ministry raised up an astonishing number of global ecumenical leaders from sister churches, such as the Churches of both South and North India. There is Ninan Koshy, who headed up International Affairs for the WCC; and Harry Daniel about whom I have written in this book. There is Wesley Ariarajah, former Director of Inter-Religious Relations for the WCC and Stanley Samartha (1926-01), whose poem appears on p. 79-81 in this book. Both blazed new paths with their theological work on Christian ministry in a pluralistic world. Echoing this same theme is K.C. Abraham, a Presbyter of the CSI, nurtured in the student world through SCM and WSCF and author of several books on the exchanges between Marxists and Indian theologians. He was adamant that faith should be rooted in the specific culture of a people, and not imported from the West. For some years he was Director of the South India Theological Research Institute in Bangalore, India which houses rows and rows of the works of M.M. Thomas. I was on that campus the night Nelson Mandela was released from prison, and remember the fireworks and celebrations. These theologians gave splendid leadership to the global community on interfaith relations at a time when the West was starting to grapple with questions of how to bear faithful Christian witness in a pluralistic society.

So the questions remain: what kind of society do we want? How do we go about achieving it? How should church and society relate? What do Christians bring to as pluralistic world where Christ crucified is not seen to be central to our common life but some of us think it is central to these questions of poverty, injustice, vulnerability, and compassion? How can we express our deepest convictions and values in the public space? India produced so many Christian leaders in response to these questions. Are we actively raising up faith leaders in our culture who can do likewise?

Harold Carlyle Wyman, Canada

27 February 1918 – 15 April 2006

Ordained United Church Minister; Ecumenist; B.A, and M.Div at United College, now University of Winnipeg ('46); Studied at Westminster College, Cambridge ('49–'50); Directed two work camps for Student Christian Movement in Canada; SCM secretary for Durham University, U.K. ('52–'53); Pastorates in Bissett and Flin Flon, MB; Grey St. United, Wpg. ('53–'60); Memorial United, St Catherines, ON ('60–'67); Cooksville United, Mississuaga, ON ('67–'84); New Zealand ('84–'85). Served on Board of Evangelism and Social Service, and Board of Christian education; After retirement shared pastorate in Brampton, ON. Married to Dorothy, three children, seven grandchildren.

It was those week long exciting days at Spring Camp with the Student Christian Movement at San Souci, Manitoba that did the trick. There we students engaged with some of the best theologians and current Christian thinkers of the day. There we met not only university student Harold Wyman, but his cohorts Peter White and Bob McLean. This triumvirate and others were leaders of a community of faith on campus that attracted others. It was a community "that welcomed those who had found in Jesus the means to the fullest realization of life, as well as those who doubted that claim and wanted to explore and question it." That's what the SCM brochure said, and several of us wanted to test it.

The context was post war Canada (the 1940s) when we realized, after the horrors of Auschwitz, and the complicity of so many Christians in Germany, that we needed to ask some hard questions about Christian faith and practice. If it was not possible to "build the Kingdom of God on earth" after all, then what was it all about? In Europe the message of the prominent theologian Karl Barth, with its heavy emphasis on God's reliable action in the world, seemed to some of us (somewhat isolated from the war in Europe) to lead to an abdication from action on our part. On the other hand, those European students who had tasted war told us they could never have persisted in the faith if it had not been for Barth's assurances of the faithfulness of God.

In the SCM we found an openness to questions about Christian life and belief, a profound seriousness, and a mixture of outrageous fun and camaraderie. It gave us permission to raise all the questions we had about Jesus, knowing we would not be roped in, laughed at, excluded or ignored. It proved more appropriate than the local church to our needs as students because it encouraged an intellectually respectable faith and focused on serious small group Bible study Moreover it was ecumenical and often featured personal visits from Christians working in other parts of the globe. We met Philippe Maury who was part of the French Underground during World War II; and Suzanne de Dietrich, who taught me by her work that a woman could be a serious Biblical scholar.

It was in this community that our passion for social justice, care for the broken-hearted, and liberty to the captives was forged. In this community we found those who wanted not only to discard obsolete faith but also to repair ruined cities. We refused just to bemoan things as they were. We found buoyant and life-giving purpose, singing, fun, flexibility, and a glimpse of redemption. Some of also found husbands, or wives!

Harold Wyman was central to this community both as a student and later as a staff resource for the Movement in the U.K. and the Director of summer "Work Camps" for the Canadian SCM, which I have described in the Anne Mutch article on p. 112 of this book. He carried all these insights into his pastoral ministry as well as into his work for the national United Church. His wife Dorothy wrote me, "In his quiet unassuming way he was able to minister with an intuitive understanding of people, complete courtesy and civility, and such generosity! But he could also stick-handle through sticky church dynamics with foresight and skill. I don't remember anyone staying permanently mad at him." He was a faithful pastor, generous companion and friend, and devoted husband and father.

I have chosen to comment on the following text read at Harold's funeral because it is so entirely appropriate for a man who was the epitome of quiet and faithful service to others.

> *And during supper Jesus, knowing that the Father had given all things into his hands, and that he had come from God and was going to God, got up from the table, took off his outer robe, and tied a towel around himself. Then he poured water into a basin and began to wash the disciples' feet and to wipe them with the towel that was tied around him. He came to Simon Peter, who said to him, "Lord are you going to wash my feet?" Jesus answered, "You do not know now what I am doing but later you will understand." Peter said to him, "You will never wash my feet." Jesus said, "Unless I wash you, you have no share with me." Simon Peter said to him, "Lord, not my feet only but also my hands and my head." ...After he had washed their feet, had put on his robe, and had returned to the table, he said to them, "Do you know what I have done to you? You call me Teacher and Lord—and you are right, for that is what I am. So if I, your Lord and Teacher, have washed your feet, you ought also to wash one another's feet. For I have set you an example, that you should also do as I have done to you."*
>
> (John 13.2b-9, 12-15 NRSV)

This portrayal of Jesus is one amongst many. There is the babe in the manger, the twelve year-old boy questioning the leaders at the Jerusalem temple, the teacher in conflict at the Nazareth synagogue with local people, the healer, and the one who set his face steadfastly to Jerusalem. Here is Jesus the servant, in an act of radical hospitality, washing the feet of his disciples and urging them to do likewise to each other. John's gospel is the only one with no account of the Last Supper. Instead of writing "Jesus took the cup," we find John writing, "Jesus took a towel." In the night in which he realized his work was done ("He was going to God.") he reiterates and reinforces the Servant theme from the prophet Isaiah, chapters 49 and 50. This passage is found only in John's gospel. We might well ask why? And why does it put it in this place?

The omission of the account of the Last Supper is arresting. John was a mystic and could easily be expected to have talked about eating the flesh and drinking the blood. But he never mentions this. Why? By the time John's gospel was written, the Last Supper would have been regarded by many with a variety of interpretations. Was it a fetish? Especially holy? Magical? Necessary to take every day? Better to celebrate infrequently to preserve its "specialness?" As a teen, I remember asking my Dad what this sacrament meant, and he wisely replied that it would take me a lifetime to meditate and ponder that question.

In John's time it was possible to misunderstand the meaning of the bread and wine and many may have been already doing so. His text emphasizes servanthood as a posture of life wrought in us, by the cross, by the Spirit, by a towel. Harold's wife Dorothy writes, "When I chose this passage I was consciously comparing it with the "broken body and shed blood" so identified with the Last Supper and velcroed through much of church history with atonement and forgiveness, with Christ going to his death, with his dying, with our "salvation." But in this scene he is demonstrating how we are to give our living—and to whom! This collection of disciples was a fairly scruffy lot. I keep looking at the famous painting of this scene in the Art Gallery of Ontario, by Tintoretto."

Leonardo Da Vinci's painting of this same scene has the disciples "radiating away from Christ in almost mathematical symmetry," whereas in Tintoretto's painting the same event becomes active and dramatic as the disciples (who are all talking to each other) are joined by a band of angels, and there is a poor female servant in the foreground. The painting could well be called "The Feast of the Poor" rather than "The Last Supper." This painting raises questions.

People are hungry because they are poor. They haven't enough money to buy food. However, places such as the Community Food Centre in Toronto are now helping them to join with others to grow, cook, eat and learn about healthy foods, and advocate for political changes. Does any congregation that supplies food to people in need (food banks, Christmas hampers) have any business doing so unless it is also working actively to change public policies on food? How can the contemporary Christian church become a church that stoops to wash the feet of the downtrodden and defeated? That is a question that needs to be deeply pondered because it is so central to the authenticity and identity of the vocation of Christians in our time.

Conclusion

I have written of forty "saints" and the scripture texts read at their funeral. In most cases, as Walter Brueggemann puts it, the passage "does not require 'interpretation' or 'application' so that it can be brought near our experience and circumstance. Rather, the text is so powerful and compelling...that it requires we submit our experience to it and thereby enter our experience on new terms, namely the terms of the text."[1] In other words, it is the current situation of the reader that needs to be informed by the ancient text.

So much depends upon our openness and comprehension:

> If we fail to hear [the Biblical] text...we shall miss the summons home, the faint beginnings of new laughter in Jerusalem, and shall still be submitting to the empire, when we could be on our way rejoicing....Without the text we are at the mercy of powerful ideology, of misrepresenting propaganda, of anxiety that makes us conformist, and despair that drives us to brutality. It is precisely the text...that dismisses ideology, exposes propaganda, overrides anxiety, and offers forgiveness in the place of brutality.[2]

I hope then that you will really hear these texts, so that you will be motivated to meditate on the legacy of these forty "saints" and the scriptural passages that have pinpointed their spiritual legacy and required a new interpretation of your situation.

The story of Israel and its saints is not only about individuals. Indeed, it is primarily about a community of faith. I have therefore included three reflections on Christian community and its experience in three tragic situations seen through my eyes as I visited the site of the Bergen-Belsen concentration camp in Germany; Hiroshima in Japan; and the place of the Kwangju Massacre in South Korea. In all three cases I went with international partners drawn from the World Council of Churches. These short pieces honour the untold and unidentified "saints" of those historic catastrophes. They too may suggest ways for us to reorder our lives and our priorities.

BERGEN-BELSEN, GERMANY

Visit by Members of Central Committee of the World Council of Churches to site of Bergen-Belsen concentration camp, 17 August 1988

I was part of that delegation, and still have searing memories of that day. It was not just the fact of standing on the actual historical place where so many atrocities had been committed. It was not just to know that Anna Frank, who was about my age and whose story I had known since I was twelve years of age, died here. It was not just to visit the documentation centre which provided me with an insight into the unimaginable conditions of the camp and the political conditions behind its development. It was to have a Jewish rabbi lead worship with Christians whose churches at the time had not acknowledged the irony of the crucifixion they had enacted in this camp.

There are no more barbed wires or barracks to bear witness to the dreadful events of the past, no evidence left of the crematorium where once a week a truck from a nearby chemical plant would pick up the remaining bones of the burnt victims of the camp and make soap out of them. On 21 May 1945, when the disease ridden camp had been completely evacuated, the British Army set the last hut on fire with a flame thrower and burnt it to the ground to eradicate the germs and stop the epidemics. Thus Bergen-Belsen, in use since 1943, disappeared from the face of the earth. What has remained are the clusters of beautiful birch trees, the mass graves in the heath, and the memorial established to help us remember the thousands of mortally ill and emaciated people so exhausted by hunger and disease that they continued to die in great numbers during the days and weeks following liberation. Anna Frank, who had died in March 1945 of typhoid fever, had been kept in the Small Women's Camp where 8,000 women were cooped up in 12 dilapidated, typhus-infested marquees. Here people were expected to die of disease, epidemics, and hunger. And they did.[3]

Since the Central Committee of the WCC was meeting in nearby Hamburg, this day was arranged for us to anchor ourselves in the reality of injustice and suffering we so often addressed in our resolutions. We had come from every nation on the earth, and represented over 349 denominations and churches. There was Walter Makula from South Africa; Johannes Hempel from East Germany; Marga Bührig from Switzerland; Nita Barrow from Barbados; Paulos Gregorius from India; Ofelia Ortega from Cuba; Dr. Nababan from Indonesia; Emilio Castro from Uruguay....the list went on and on. We gathered to remember those who, after liberation on 15 April 1945 by British troops, died of disease or malnutrition. We gathered to remember those who survived the concentration camp but whose health was so seriously affected that despite medical care, they experienced the tragedy of being liberated but still condemned to die as victims of a ruthless regime.

Remembrance was evoked with a service. We began with a commemoration of the dead at the Soviet Cemetery, led by Archbishop Kirill of Smolensk (now Patriarch of the Russian Orthodox Church). Many Soviet soldiers had been sent to Bergen-Belsen as Prisoners of War, and they then died of hunger and disease. This was followed by a walk through lovely birches to the obelisk and Wall of Inscriptions of names built on the grounds of the former concentration camp, where a silent meditation was held, and each of us placed a memorial candle in front of the wall. From there we walked to the Jewish Memorial, where the following verses were sung and read from this version of Psalm 22 by Cantor Emil Levy and Regional Rabbi Henry G. Brandt. Flowers were laid.

> *My God, my God, why have you deserted me? How far from saving me, the words I groan! I call all day, my God, but you never answer, all night long I call and cannot rest. Yet, Holy One, you who make your home in the praises of Israel, in you our fathers put their trust, they trusted and you rescued them. They called to you for help and they were saved, they never trusted you in vain.*
>
> *Yet here I am, now more worm than man, scorn of making, jest of the people, all who see me jeer at me. (...) Do not stand aside, trouble is near. I have no one to help me! (...) and my tongue is stuck to my jaw. A pack of dogs surround me, a gang of villains closes me in; they tie me hand and foot and leave me lying in the dust of death.*
>
> *I can count every one of my bones, and there they glare at me, gloating; they divide my garments among them and cast lots for my clothes. Do not stand aside Yahweh. O my strength, come quickly to my help; rescue my soul from the sword (...)*

What a *cri de coeur*. The pain is palpable; the images threatening. Why did God not even hear the groans of the suffering ones? Why was God so silent in the midst of the enormous physical, psychological, and social suffering to which Bergen-Belsen bore witness? The psalmist expresses the desolation, pain and abandonment of the victims beaten up, tortured and destroyed by "a pack of dogs." The pain is comparable to the destruction of Jerusalem for Jews, and the Crucifixion for Christians. It is the dark night of the soul: "Night," of which Elie Weisel wrote.

Yet even while experiencing the absence and silence of God the psalmist is ambivalent, and cries out to one who was known as trustworthy. He remembers that "our fathers trusted and you rescued them...they never trusted you in vain." Karl Barth is reported as saying that prayer causes God to do things that God would not otherwise do. I wonder about that. Here the psalmist, who knows one can find God in the midst of suffering, cries out for deliverance. Suddenly the psalm shifts direction, and ends with praise for the One who has not hidden his face, but is fully present and has answered, even in the midst of despair.

> *Then I shall proclaim your name to my brothers. Praise you in full assembly (...) for he has not despised or disdained the poor man in his poverty, has not hidden his face from him, but has answered him when he called. O that thou wouldst hear me, O Lord. Amen.*

Are we able to relate to this experience at all? Perhaps those who have experienced a sudden diagnosis of terminal cancer, or a failed marriage, or relentless ongoing poverty are more able than the rest who continue to respond "I am fine" to every inquiry. The psalm bears witness to the fact that suffering is a place where one can find God. Can this be true for the sole family survivors in war torn Syria, or the dismembered and discarded aboriginal "missing" women in Canada? Recently the General Secretary of the WCC visited Council Fire, Toronto, where he met with aboriginal peoples and others. In the middle of his speech about ecumenism, he was interrupted by a woman in the back of the hall who cried out, "Where was God when the Archbishop of Albany raped me?" The hall fell silent.

Recently a group of young people were talking about their experience of God, and two of them said it was out on a lake, certainly in the outdoors, that they knew God. What has that to do with the experience of Bergen-Belsen? Certainly they experienced awe, but it seemed a long way from finding God in suffering. What about those who are "spiritual" but not "religious?" What would they make of this psalm and its profound movement from desolation and suffering to confidence?

But let us continue our visit at Bergen-Belsen. We then walked to the Documents Hall, which has preserved as many documents as possible. Some of them are diaries of Jews from the Netherlands and Mediterranean countries who were imprisoned in readiness to be exchanged for German prisoners abroad. Here were imprisoned the most seriously ill prisoners from other camps in the

"Reich." We were reminded too, of the many gay and lesbian people condemned to death by the regime. One of my colleagues from the USA, whose faith had not prepared her for the horror, couldn't bear to read these documents or view the pictorial history, so she stayed outside the building until we were all finished.

From there we proceeded to the Cemetery of those who died after liberation. Worship was led at this site by Bishop Horst Hirschler of the Evangelical Lutheran Church of Hanover, and Archbishop John Habgood of York, UK. The latter read the Beatitudes (Matthew 5.3–10 RSV):

> *Blessed are those who mourn, for they shall be comforted…Blessed are the peacemakers, for they shall be called the children of God.…Blessed are those who are persecuted for righteousness' sake, for theirs is the kingdom of heaven.*

Prayers were offered and we sang, "Christ is now risen again, from his death and all his pain; therefore will we thankful be, and rejoice with him gladly. Hallelujah!

On this occasion, members of the Central Committee of the WCC were from many countries, including the previously warring countries of Germany and USSR. They joined together in a Christian service of reconciliation, remembrance of their dead, and prayers for peace. They committed themselves once more to moving through crucifixion to resurrection, through despair to hope, through desolation to transformation. In short, to living the Christian story.

I am reminded of the disturbing words spoken by Protestant pastor Martin Niemöller, who had initially supported Nazism, but soon realized his mistake and was arrested in 1937 and imprisoned in Dachau for his opposition to the regime. His searing words expressing the danger of political apathy resonate with us today:

> *First they came for the Communists. I didn't speak out because I was not a Communist. Then they came for the Socialists, and I didn't speak out because I was not a Socialist. Then they came for the Trade Unionists, and I didn't speak out because I was not a Trade Unionist. Then they came for the Jews, and I didn't speak out because I am not a Jew. Then they came for me. And there was no one left to speak out for me.*

Hiroshima, Japan

"Atomic bomb dropped at 8.15 am on 6 August 1945, 580 meters above the centre of Hiroshima, causing incalculable human and material destruction." (From Hiroshima Peace Garden Museum)

Students in school uniforms and sleek white cars were touring the site. The surrounding hills were aflame in autumn colours. Everything seemed so normal. At 8.15 am after breakfast with a friend from Thailand, I had walked to the centre of Hiroshima where the Atomic Bomb had been dropped forty-two years earlier. At the junction of two rivers and a small bridge over the Oba River, I suddenly saw the burnt out silhouette of the building that had been at the very centre of the blast. Rivers had been polluted and the landscape demolished. All that remained were the skeletal bones of the building, stark against the silent blue sky. It was no accident that Hiroshima was targeted during the war, as it was the base of the Second General Headquarters of the Imperial Japanese Army, and an enormous container of mustard gas had been buried under the city. This did not diminish the horror of the A-bomb, but it did put it in historical perspective for me.

I visited Hiroshima in November 1987 as a delegate to a consultation of the World Council of Churches on "Peace, Justice, and the Integrity of Creation" convened in Osaka, Japan. My Korean guide took us across the river to the Peace Garden and Memorial to the victims, which I found deeply disturbing. There I found the mural "Descent into Hell," the fountain of peace, the eternal flame, and the cenotaph recording many, many names of Japanese victims. But not the names of Korean victims. Their memorial was not allowed to be built inside the Peace Garden, as they were considered "aliens" in Japan. Their monument is a small one across the river, erected on 10 April 1970. No funerals and no medical services were provided for them, although 10% of the victims of the bomb were Korean. It was particularly difficult as many Buddhist Koreans, who had been forced to work in Japan during the war, believed there was no rest for the soul until they have been properly memorialized. I felt a tension at Hiroshima between the universal aspiration of the Peace Memorial and the exclusion of non-Japanese victims. Of the 100,000 Koreans who were in Japan in 1945, 30,000 returned to Korea, where over 10,000 had since died, mostly of the effects of radiation, while others suffered the after-effects of either blood cancer or sterility.

I attended the Kyodan Hiroshima Fuchu Church on Sunday, and heard first-hand the experiences of the "Hibakusha"—the survivors. The presiding minster had been 1.3 kms from the centre when the bomb dropped. He was lucky to have suffered only a crushed arm and acute leukemia, unlike the persons who were vaporized while sitting on the steps of the Bank. All that now remained of them were the white outlines and imprints of what used to be human beings. I though immediately of the white chalk outlines of human beings that peace activists in Toronto had scrawled on the dark pavement outside my house on Hiroshima Day. I was completely wiped out after listening to the devastating stories of the survivors. I was told it was not good to be known as a victim, as fear of genetic defects could affect your prospects for marriage and jobs. Social damage of the bomb included disruption of families, neighbourhoods and disintegration of communities.

I admired the wreath of peace adorning the 1958 children's peace monument in Hiroshima Peace Park. On the pedestal of the monument stands a life size image of Sadako, a young Japanese girl who was two years old when the bomb was dropped. Although she was a strong athletic girl, at age eleven, while practicing for a relay race, she felt dizzy and fell. She was diagnosed with leukemia. Her friend brought her a gold paper crane and told her of an old Japanese legend, which says that anyone who folds a thousand paper cranes will be granted a wish. Sadako completed over 1,000 cranes before making her wish for peace, and then dying on 25 October 1955, at age twelve. On the monument, her hands raised to the sky, she holds a golden paper crane. The paper crane has become an international symbol of peace as a result of this girl's courage, and I remembered learning to make them so long ago at church camps in Canada.

I left at the Garden at 3:30 pm, filled with rage. I wrote in my diary, "Here the Christian church has nurtured a bunch of illiterates who think other things have priority over peace. There's too much suffering. I have seen the graves of Leningrad; the ghetto in Budapest: the Argentinean Mothers of May Square; the sunken vessels in Pearl Harbour; the kids with no shoes in Uruguay. All Christians do is talk, and all Peace Research Institutes do is publish research papers. We simply must identify a common action for Christians, as a public witness, and lay the Biblical foundation so it becomes obvious that peace between peoples is the primary requirement of our faith. I would so like to be part of an historical movement to win peace and justice for people." That day in Hiroshima, the absence of God was palpable to me.

Through it all, some Christians were at work. Rev. Tad Mitsui, a United Church minister, told me this wonderful ecumenical story. Twenty-five female victims who had experienced the destruction and distortion of their faces because of the bomb faced a bleak future. There could be no hope of marriage, and that meant total social marginalization. Rev. Tanimoto, a Methodist minister, who had studied theology in the USA before World War II, was a friend of journalist Norman Cousins. Together they organized a trip for the "Hiroshima maidens" to the USA for restorative plastic surgery. Tanimoto had travelled from Hiroshima to Tokyo with the women and was met by Tad's father, Rev. Isamu Mitsui, who arranged housing for the 25 women in Tokyo while they were waiting to receive their papers for the USA. The women were billeted in the homes of Mitsui's church members. Upon arrival in the USA, the women were hosted by Quakers and Jewish families in 1955–56 while undergoing surgery and recovery. While in the USA, Cousins arranged for a TV appearance on *This is Your Life*, although the women appeared only as silhouettes behind a screen. This was one of the very few times Americans had immediate access to survivors of the Atomic bomb in the decades following the war.[4]

The Feast of the Transfiguration for the Eastern, Syrian and Indian Orthodox churches, the Episcopal Anglican churches, and others always falls on 6 August. It is one of the major feasts among the twelve great feasts of Orthodoxy that has been widely observed since the fourth century. It is sometimes referred to as the Small Epiphany, as the Father speaks from beyond, the Son is transformed, and the Holy Spirit appears as a cloud. The baptism of Jesus, the Great Epiphany, records the same actions. This day in August is also the Anniversary of the Hiroshima bombing. On 6 August 1983 at the World Council of Churches Assembly in Vancouver, Philip Potter, General Secretary of the WCC, led a meditation on the Transfiguration.

> *Six days later, Jesus took with him Peter and James and his brother John and led them up a high mountain, by themselves. And he was transfigured before them, and his face shone like the sun, and his clothes became dazzling white. Suddenly there appeared to them Moses and Elijah, talking with him. Then Peter said to Jesus, "Lord it is good for us to be here; if you wish, I will make three dwellings here, one for you, one for Moses, and one for Elijah." While he was still speaking, suddenly a bright cloud overshadowed them, and from the cloud a voice said, "This is my Son, the Beloved; with him I am well pleased; listen to him!" When the disciples heard, this they fell to the ground and were overcome with fear. But Jesus came and touched them, saying, "Get up and do not be*

afraid." And when they looked up, they saw no one except Jesus himself alone.
(Matthew 17.1-8, NRSV)

The accounts of both the Hiroshima bombing and the Transfiguration share certain elements: a blinding white light; a roar; a cloud; the shock factor of horror and terror; instantaneous clarity of vision; and a flashpoint of a fundamentally changed world. Hiroshima transformed the world through destruction. The Transfiguration transfigured it and revealed God's purposes for a loving, justice-filled, and environmentally secure world, through the person and work of Jesus Christ. Potter referred to the way the Transfiguration disclosed another world: "We represent all that went into the decision regarding the bombing of Hiroshima and Nagasaki, and also its effects in death and destruction. Our worship here, our testimonies have enabled us to glimpse again the transformed, transfigured being of Christ, the bringer of peace and righteousness—justice...Only in him and through him can we take an unequivocal stand for peace and justice...we enter into the sufferings of the world as we share the sufferings of Christ."[5]

The WCC Assembly went to work and overwhelming passed a resolution stating their belief that "the production and deployment as well as the use of nuclear weapons are a crime against humanity, and...such activities must be condemned on ethical and theological grounds." This statement and action resonated around the world, particularly with secular colleagues. Thirty years ago, it committed Christian churches all around the world to taking action to establish peace. It certainly propelled me into action.

It's easier to pass a resolution than to take action requiring analysis, building trust, and long term relationships and to advocate for a nuclear free world. There is still no world consensus or mandatory verifiable international treaty on the banning of all nuclear weapons, despite a worldwide signature campaign on the Internet, and ongoing vigorous efforts in Canada led by former Senator Douglas Roche. What steps can you take to further this initiative? How has your church taken action on peace? How much is universal peace a priority for you? Your congregation? Your country?

City of Kwangju, South Korea
May 1980

A team visit of delegates of the Central Committee of the World Council of Churches to the site of the Kwangju Massacre in January 1981.

"I was taken to the YWCA in Kwangju where I saw bullet holes in the walls and ceilings of the first floor. The corner drainpipe was dark with splattered blood that had leaked down from the second floor, turned into a morgue. He was nineteen," said the father of one of the murdered students as we sat together with thirty other fathers and mothers who had defied martial law and travelled long distances to meet with me who represented the international Christian community. "The night we heard the shooting downtown, we urged our son not to go and join the fighting...not that night. But he insisted that that night, of all nights, he must go. It could mean the restoration of democracy to South Korea."[6]

Clearly, an illegal act was called for, even though I had not done too many illegal things in my life up to this point. Our 1981 WCC delegation to South Korea had been received at the Christian Building in Seoul. As I was the only woman in the delegation, I was approached by two women at that reception who insisted that I visit the provincial town of Kwangju, site of a reported massacre of students. The country, under the dictatorship of Chun Doo Hwan, was under martial law, and travel outside Seoul was strictly forbidden. I decided to respond to the desperate plea of the two women despite it being illegal. At the last minute the head of our delegation, Dr. Konrad Raiser of the WCC, had whispered to me, "If you go to Kwangju, I'll support you." That was all I needed to hear. Despite the fact that both the Korean Government and our partner churches in Korea advised against such a visit, I caught a train to Kwangju with the help of Walter Beecham, a missionary for the United Church. He knew the language, the people, the difficulties, and the risks.

Margaret Atwood has written, "The facts of this world seen clearly / are seen through tears; / why tell me then / there is something wrong with my eyes?"[7] At Kwangju I saw the world through tears.

I was met at the train station in Kwangju by Rev. Kang Shin Seok, a minister of the Presbyterian Church in the Republic of Korea, a partner of the United Church of Canada. At first Kwangju looked to me like any other city in South Korea, until I began to notice some oddities. We visited a Presbyterian church with no minister, because he had gone into hiding after the massacre, and "Wanted" posters for him were posted all over Korea. When I met his wife who had no idea if he was dead or alive, I could not tell her (for security reasons) that I had visited her husband two days previously hiding in an attic in Seoul. The Baptist minister we met took me to the hospital to talk to those who had first been alerted to the massacre by the non-stop number of corpses that kept arriving that fatal night in May 1980. The official government count of corpses, which of course minimized the extent of the massacre, was much less than the actual count of bodies, documented by this Baptist minister.

Over breakfast in his modest home, Kang told me the story, later confirmed by many others. Following a peaceful demonstration of 20,000 students for a return to democracy on 6 May 1980, Korean paratroopers, drunk on rice wine moved in. They were supported by the USA, which did not want to lose its military base in South Korea, and imagined a communist behind every incident of citizen protest. The Korean troops began murdering students, old people, children, and workers. Tragically, it was Korean against Korean. Hundreds were butchered in the streets. Bodies littered the streets and hospitals were overflowing with dead and injured. Some were brutally beaten never to work again. Faced with this brutal attack on unarmed citizens, the whole city rose up to resist the slaughter and temporarily drove the military out of the city. On 27 May at 2:00 a.m., the tide turned. More than 17,000 heavily armed Korean troops stormed the city with helicopters and gunned down all resisters. Some had fingernails torn out to force a confession that they were anti-government Communists. The government did not believe that they were Christians, working to restore democracy. Many people simply disappeared, never to be seen again. Later, the Government threatened the minister who hosted me, and when they discovered he had gone into hiding, went after his teen-aged son. Kang had to leave his place of hiding so they would release his son, and he laughingly told me a few years later that they gave him a two-year jail sentence. And all on my account!

When we left the YWCA to visit the cemetery that day, the taxi driver would not accept our fare. "My son," he said," received only a life sentence, not death, not execution." I was astonished by the ways people shared incredible agony, incredible courage, and incredible strength. We travelled muddy roads past the infamous Kwangju prison where so many students and ministers had served "time." No heat in those tiny prison cells, but the cheerful bell from the Buddhist Temple continued to greet each new day. Little girls waves as we passed the rice fields. Finally we arrived at the gravesites. Men at work digging a nearby grave carted the clay away in huge wicker baskets. A father who had lost his son asked me to say a prayer at the graveside. But I couldn't. I was spiritually paralyzed by a sharp sense of the absence of God, and I pleaded, "Will you pray for me?"

As it turned out, the citizen uprising in Kwangju turned out to be an historical dividing line in Korean history. Lives were not lost in vain, pro-democracy forces were consolidated; plans for a democratic future were embraced. The event opened up a new road for the nation. Korean history took a new turn and the country re-emerged when the pro-democracy leader Kim Dae-Jung was eventually elected President.

On the twentieth anniversary of the massacre in 2000, the former political prisoner, now President of Korea, Kim Dae-Jung (see p. 32 of this book), mounted a celebration. To that event he invited representatives from churches and countries from around the world that had supported the pro-democracy struggle. Sang Chul Lee (former Moderator of the United Church of Canada) and I were fortunate to be invited to the memorial service at the National Cemetery, where the martyrs were honoured. Korea had never forgotten that the Canadian Parliament had passed a resolution that had pleaded clemency for the life of Kim Dae-Jung in 1980 when he had been given the death penalty by Dictator Chun Doo Hwan. Resonating in my head was that passage from Hebrews 11.32–38 (NRSV):

> *And what more should I say? For time would fail me to tell of Gideon, Barak, Samson, Jephthah, of David and Samuel and the prophets—who through faith conquered kingdoms, administered justice, obtained promises, shut the mouths of lions, quenched raging fire, escaped the edge of the sword, won strength out of weakness...[Some] were tortured, refusing to accept release...Others suffered mocking and flogging, and even chains and imprisonment. They were stoned to death, they were sawn in two, they were killed by the sword; they went about... destitute, persecuted, tormented—of whom the world was not worthy.*

I added, "and the martyrs of Kwangju." When I returned to peaceful Canada, I wrote in my diary, "What is the meaning of undeserved suffering? Is it the birth pangs of a new creation?" I have no clear answer. But I do know that out of this resistance to the death came a new democratic order in Korea, and that remains the legacy of the Kwangju martyrs. The cost of discipleship was very high.

In 2010 I represented the United Church at the General Assembly of the Presbyterian Church in the Republic of Korea (South Korea). During the dictatorship it was said of this church, "they all believe in Jesus, but expect to go to prison," to distinguish them from other churches of whom it was said, "They believe in Jesus and expect to go to heaven." Some of my former colleagues arranged a dinner in my honor and we had a rich reunion. Oh Jae Shik, Park Hyung-Kyu, Kang Moon-Kyu, and Lee Sang Chul were all there, and I recalled their courageous work and witness. I want to be in that number!

The suffering and high cost of discipleship continues in other parts of the world. Members of the Coptic Orthodox Church in Egypt have suffered minority status for many years. For many years anyone who converted to Christian faith and was caught and identified was made to stamp and trample on an image of Jesus. When I was President of the WCC, one of the Coptic Archbishops pleaded with me then to try to get some of the recent converts accepted as refugees in Canada. Today, Christians are currently experiencing intensification of their marginalization, which is now turning into persecution in the newly emerging state. Fortunately, progressive Muslims support them, but they are in the minority within their own faith group.

What is the cost of being a Christian in Canada today? José Miguez Bonino of Argentina had some disturbing ideas. He suggested that one of problems of some Western and Northern churches was their alliance of mission with Western ideology and expansion, which in his view, distorted the priorities of the gospel "beyond recognition...missions speak about numbers...the number of converts, the number of churches, the number of congregations, and so on." But there are other issues at stake. "Your church, your money, your people will either reinforce the pattern of domination and exploitation [we experience in Latin America] or participate in the struggle" for the liberation of people from all that robs them of their full humanity.[8] I wonder what he would have thought of Venezuela's Chavez and his popularity with the poor of his country?

What does it mean for Christians called to be increasingly countercultural in our context? Will the institutional church lend support to those who take that path? In this regard what path do you see the new Pope taking? Does it matter? What are the implications for us as our religious institutions decline in influence and numbers? What are the options? Flee the institution? Renew it? What initiatives can we be taking inside, alongside or outside the institution to make the gospel incarnate in our culture?

Endnotes

1   Walter Brueggemann, *A Commentary on Jeremiah: Exile and Homecoming* (Grand Rapids, MI/Cambridge, UK: William B. Eerdmans Publishing Company, 1998), p. 18.

2   Walter Brueggemann, *A Commentary on Jeremiah*, pp. 18-19.

3   Many details come from Eberhard Kolb, *Bergen-Belsen: From 1943 to 1945* (Göttingen: Vandenhoeck and Ruprecht, 1986).

4   Rodney Barker, *The Hiroshima Maidens: A Story of Courage, Compassion, and Survival* (NY: Viking Press,1985).

5   WCC Sixth Assembly, Vancouver, 1983 in *One World,* A Monthly Magazine of the World Council of Churches, No. 89 (Geneva, Switzerland: Communications Department of WCC, 1983), pp. 4, 9-10.

6   From the 1981 diary of Lois M. Wilson.

7   Margaret Atwood, "Notes towards a Poem that can never be Written (for Carolyn Forché)," *Selected Poems II: Poems Selected and New 1976–1986* (Boston: Houghton Mifflin, 1987), pp. 71-74.

8   José Miguez Bonino, *Mission as Conflict and Challenge,* n. pag.

Christmas, 1960

No traveller that the world has known
Has journeyed anywhere alone
But takes for company
— All saints.

Invited or unbidden,
Openly or hidden,
They follow on the way.

Then cheer your hearts, lift up your voice
In praise to God this day;
Whatever road your feet have trod,
—Smooth, rough, broad or narrow,
See! Glimpsed by star-light,
Or heard in a wisp of song,
The endless generations of God,
Beckoning you along!

— R.K.N. McLean, a cool saint from Manitoba.
(kindly provided by Dorothy Wyman)

Other books by the author

Like a Mighty River
1981, WoodLake Press, Winfield, BC

Turning The World Upside Down
1989, Doubleday Canada Limited, Toronto

Telling Her Story
1992, The United Church of Canada Publishing House, Toronto

Miriam, Mary and Me
1996, Northstone Publishing, Kelowna, BC

Stories Seldom Told
1997, Northstone Publishing, Kelowna, BC

Nuclear Waste, Exporing the Ethical Dilemmas
2000, The United Church Publishing House

Streams of Faith
2006, The United Church Publishing House, Toronto.